CAMBRIDGE
UNIVERSITY PRESS

Cambridge IGCSE™ and O Level
Global Perspectives

COURSEBOOK

Keely Laycock, Frances Nehme-Pearson & Fleur McLennan

CAMBRIDGE
UNIVERSITY PRESS & ASSESSMENT

Shaftesbury Road, Cambridge CB2 8EA, United Kingdom

One Liberty Plaza, 20th Floor, New York, NY 10006, USA

477 Williamstown Road, Port Melbourne, VIC 3207, Australia

314–321, 3rd Floor, Plot 3, Splendor Forum, Jasola District Centre, New Delhi – 110025, India

103 Penang Road, #05–06/07, Visioncrest Commercial, Singapore 238467

Cambridge University Press & Assessment is a department of the University of Cambridge.

We share the University's mission to contribute to society through the pursuit of education, learning and research at the highest international levels of excellence.

www.cambridge.org
Information on this title: www.cambridge.org/9781009301428

First published 2016
Second edition 2023
20 19 18 17 16 15 14 13 12 11 10 9 8 7 6 5 4 3 2 1

Printed in Italy by L.E.G.O. S.p.A.

A catalogue record for this publication is available from the British Library

ISBN   978-1-009-30142-8   Coursebook Print & GO
ISBN   978-1-009-30143-5   Digital Coursebook (2 Years)
ISBN   978-1-009-30141-1   eBook

Additional resources for this publication at www.cambridge.org/go

Endorsement statement

Endorsement indicates that a resource has passed Cambridge International's rigorous quality-assurance process and is suitable to support the delivery of a Cambridge International syllabus. However, endorsed resources are not the only suitable materials available to support teaching and learning, and are not essential to be used to achieve the qualification. Resource lists found on the Cambridge International website will include this resource and other endorsed resources.

Any example answers to questions taken from past question papers, practice questions, accompanying marks and mark schemes included in this resource have been written by the authors and are for guidance only. They do not replicate examination papers. In examinations the way marks are awarded may be different. Any references to assessment and/or assessment preparation are the publisher's interpretation of the syllabus requirements. Examiners will not use endorsed resources as a source of material for any assessment set by Cambridge International.

While the publishers have made every attempt to ensure that advice on the qualification and its assessment is accurate, the official syllabus, specimen assessment materials and any associated assessment guidance materials produced by the awarding body are the only authoritative source of information and should always be referred to for definitive guidance. Cambridge International recommends that teachers consider using a range of teaching and learning resources based on their own professional judgement of their students' needs.

Cambridge International has not paid for the production of this resource, nor does Cambridge International receive any royalties from its sale. For more information about the endorsement process, please visit www.cambridgeinternational.org/endorsed-resources

Cambridge International copyright material in this publication is reproduced under licence and remains the intellectual property of Cambridge Assessment International Education.

Third party websites and resources referred to in this publication have not been endorsed by Cambridge Assessment International Education.

› Contents

> Introduction

This book is for all learners studying Cambridge IGCSE™ and O Level Global Perspectives, and anyone else who wants to develop their information skills, critical thinking, independent learning, collaboration and communication skills, using global topics and issues to practise these skills.

What is Cambridge IGCSE and O Level Global Perspectives?

Cambridge IGCSE and O Level Global Perspectives gives you the opportunity to think about significant global issues and to consider these from different angles, including personal, local, national and global perspectives. The active learning approach used in the course puts you at the centre of the learning and encourages you to think hard about how you learn, not just about what you learn. It will support you to make your own decisions independently and build your own understanding of the topics, issues and skills undertaken. Furthermore, you will develop responsibility for your own learning by considering, planning and accomplishing tasks and actions.

The focus of the course is on skills rather than content. Research, analysis, evaluation, communication, collaboration and reflection are the core skills that underpin the structure of the course. By developing your skills in constructing arguments, presenting views, working collaboratively, conducting research, and reasoning and reflecting on your place in a connected world, you will build on the core skills which support and enhance learning in other subjects. Since these skills are transferable and ongoing, they also prepare you for further study, future employment opportunities and lifelong learning.

What do you do in a Cambridge IGCSE and O Level Global Perspectives course?

In your lifetime, we will face some global challenges that do not have easy or quick solutions. These include how to best live sustainably, now and in the future, as well as coping with a rapidly changing world that will have an impact on your life chances and choices. Other challenges involve technology and how to navigate an increasingly connected and information-rich world, while also understanding more about yourself and how to gain a sense of your own active place in the world.

Cambridge IGCSE and O Level Global Perspectives focuses on skill development using some of the inspiring and engaging global topics and issues from the syllabus, although any topic or issue could be used to acquire and develop the skills. You will demonstrate your learning by applying the skills – or the 'how to learn' – rather than by aquiring and presenting knowledge. Showing how learning is developing is undertaken in a different way from most curriculum areas. It involves building up your confidence and ability with the core skill and then applying it in a variety of ways. There are also opportunities to go deeper into topics and skills to follow your own personal interests.

Each chapter of this book focuses on a particular skill set that you will need to develop over the Cambridge IGCSE and O Level Global Perspectives course, including:

- researching, analysing and evaluating information
- developing and justifying a line of reasoning
- reflecting on processes and on own learning
- communicating information and reasoning
- collaborating to achieve a common outcome.

Our approach in Cambridge IGCSE and O Level Global Perspectives encourages you to be confident, responsible, reflective, innovative and engaged. This is achieved through serious consideration of the opinions, choices and decisions that you make. There is a strong focus on the use of classroom dialogue and questioning to help you develop higher order thinking skills and metacognition. Talking is one of the most effective ways to approach the course. Using discussions and asking challenging questions of yourself and those in the classroom can broaden understanding and engagement with the course. Learning how to consider others people's opinions, choices and decisions creates successful learning conditions.

Why Cambridge IGCSE and O Level Global Perspectives matters

The Cambridge IGCSE and O Level Global Perspectives course has been developed to give you the opportunity to develop the skills you will need to meet the challenges of living in the twenty-first century. You will encounter the topics in new and empathetic ways, while steering away from replicating knowledge and retrieving content. The course begins with you understanding yourself and how you learn before moving on to look at understanding other people's perspectives. Topics and learning concentrate on using empathy to understand multiple points of view. Choice and reasoning are also used to go deeper into the learning and to find a different path. The six core skills that are developed throughout the course will help you become active citizens of the future, making responsible choices for yourself, your community and the world.

The course encourages you to be more inquisitive about the world around you, become more self-directed in your learning, and use critical and creative thinking to find potential solutions to complex issues facing your own communities as well as those facing the planet.

Cambridge IGCSE and O Level Global Perspectives inspires you to engage with the uniqueness of your own local places and people, while also developing an understanding of your responsibility to the world.

Topics and how they should be explored

In your Cambridge IGCSE and O Level Global Perspectives course you will have the opportunity to think about and explore a wide variety of topics and apply the skills you learn to help you think more critically about the complexities of the modern world.

The six core skills are developed through the following topics:

- Arts in society
- Change in culture and communities
- Climate change, energy and resources
- Conflict and peace
- Development, trade and aid
- Digital world
- Education for all
- Employment
- Environment, pollution and conservation
- Globalisation
- Health and wellbeing

- Law and criminality
- Media and communication
- Migration and urbanisation
- Political power and action
- Poverty and inequality
- Social identity and inclusion
- Sport and recreation
- Technology, industry and innovation
- Transport, travel and tourism
- Values and beliefs
- Water, food and agriculture

There is no set curriculum or pathway for the topics to be taught. How and how many topics are explored are choices for your school and teachers to make. They will ensure that you explore topics with both short-term and long-term learning outcomes in mind. Topics are designed to engage and excite, so you can go further into each topic than the suggested activities and reading. Exploring the topics will build on your prior knowledge and abilities, with lots of opportunity to talk with peers and others from the community and listening to multiple perspectives. A variety of activities, such as group work and guided learning, helps build collaboration and communication skills, while individual activities encourage independence. There are lots of opportunities to support your learning with helpful tips, modelled responses, and reflections on your learning journey as you progress through the course.

Transferring skills

The skills that you will develop during this course can easily transfer to other curriculum areas. Communication skills are helpful for anyone who is also studying courses that need essay writing or presentation skills, such as English Language and Literature, Travel and Tourism or Enterprise. Similarly, the core skill of collaboration is not just for school but is a valuable skill for day-to-day interactions with people in the community.

Analysis, research and evaluation are also the core skills of many other curriculum areas, giving you the opportunity to accelerate your learning. Cambridge IGCSE and O Level Global Perspectives can also help you to prepare for assessment points and examinations through its focus on your thinking and use of metacognition. The course encourages you to be reflective on your personal strengths, while also keeping in mind areas for improvement. This can streamline study time and make revision more focused on the areas that need improving.

Studying Cambridge IGCSE and O Level Global Perspectives will provide you with a strong foundation for further studies in AS & A Level Global Perspectives & Research as well as many other Cambridge International AS & A Level subjects. It also provides you with a strong starting point for further academic studies at university level.

> How to use this book

Throughout this coursebook, you will notice recurring features that are designed to help your learning. Here is a brief overview of what you will find.

LEARNING INTENTIONS

Learning intentions start each chapter and set out what you should expect to learn by the end of the chapter, helping you to navigate the content.

BEFORE YOU START

This contains questions and activities to check your understanding before starting the chapter.

ACTIVITY

These are practical tasks that allow you to understand and apply relevant skills and perspectives to what you are learning.

REFLECTION

Reflection boxes help you to think about your learning, understand the skills you are developing and understand how you can enhance these within your learning.

SHOWCASING YOUR SKILLS

The Showcase is a larger activity at the end of each chapter to help you use all the skills you have learned in the chapter.

SUMMARY

The summaries sum up the content in each chapter and refer back to the learning intentions to help you recap the most important content within the chapter.

REVIEW AND REFLECTION

At the end of each chapter, you will find a table outlining the content that you should now understand. There is space to reflect on what you have learned about these topics and where you may need to practise more to improve your understanding.

KEY WORDS

Key words are highlighted in the text when they are first introduced. You will find definitions of these words in boxes like this near the first use, and in the glossary at the back of this book.

TIP

These give you additional helpful information and include guidance on common errors to avoid.

DISCUSSION

These are questions or activities that you can use to reflect on, in pairs or groups on the topic and what you have learned.

Note: where examples of student work are provided, these have been written by our authors.

Chapter 1

Getting started with Cambridge Global Perspectives™

LEARNING INTENTIONS

In this chapter you will:

- Understand what a perspective is

- Identify how people can have different perspectives

- Learn what is meant by a global, national, local or personal perspective

- Connect your interests to global topics

- Explore issues which are relevant to global topics

- Examine the skills you will develop as part of studying Cambridge Global Perspectives

- Begin a Cambridge Global Perspectives magazine or newsletter, which you can continue throughout the course.

Living in the twenty-first century, we are inhabitants of a world which is getting bigger and more diverse. As a result, we need to deal more than ever with complexity and understand different points of view about the world. Cambridge Global Perspectives is all about giving you the skills, attitudes and behaviours to respond to these challenges.

In this chapter, you will learn about what we mean by perspectives, and think about why people might have different perspectives on the same issue, event or idea. You will also consider in more detail the key topics of global importance in the world today, and how they might relate to your own interests and to issues which are **relevant** to your own part of the world. Finally, you will think about the importance of skills and identify the main skills which you will develop as you study Cambridge Global Perspectives.

> **KEY TERM**
>
> **relevant:** directly connected with, appropriate to.

BEFORE YOU START

Before you start this chapter, take a few minutes to assess your experiences so far and the skills you already have. This will help you to identify what you know already and track your progress as you work your way through this book and the course. Make a copy of this table and use it to rate yourself:

	A little	To some extent	A lot
I feel confident in myself to deal with the challenges that come from a complex and changing world.			
I can work out the causes and consequences of important global problems and suggest ways to deal with them.			
I can understand points of view which are not my own.			
I can work independently and as part of a group.			
I can see that people might have different opinions on the same thing.			
I feel able to accept or reject pieces of information and justify why I have done so.			

Do not worry if you have ticked 'a little' for anything as you will be learning to develop your skills and confidence in these areas as part of this course. Even if you have ticked 'a lot', you may well find that you have more to learn than you imagined.

1.1 Thinking about different perspectives

Realising that we might see things differently from others is key to understanding what a **perspective** is. Perspectives are based on personal experiences of the world and thinking about them. People see the world differently because experiences and ways of thinking differ.

KEY TERM

perspective: a viewpoint on an issue based on evidence and reasoning.

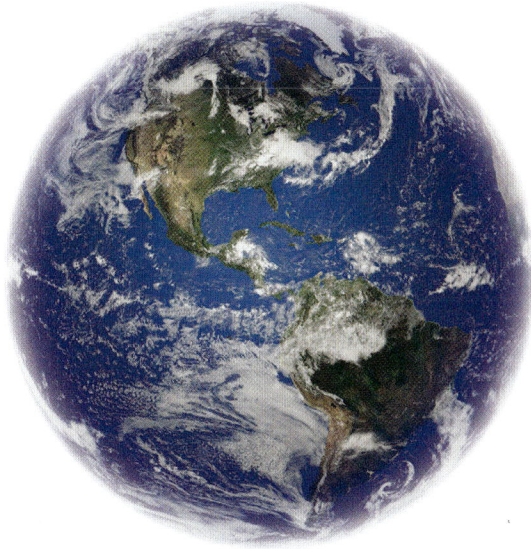

Figure 1.1: A global perspective

ACTIVITY 1.01

1   Imagine you are a passenger in a car that stops at some traffic lights. As you are waiting, a limousine pulls up at the lights. Who do you think is in the limousine?

Figure 1.2: Who do you think is in this limousine?

2   Share your ideas with the class (you could write them on a whiteboard).

The chances are that other people's ideas are different from yours: they see it from a different perspective.

When you are thinking about perspectives, it is important to consider the terms that are used to discuss them. We can sometimes think that certain words mean the same thing to everyone. We are wrong to **assume** this, which is why it's important to check meanings with others.

KEY TERM

assume: to think something is true or is certain to happen, without checking if we are right.

ACTIVITY 1.02

Here are three words. They are all topics/parts of topics in the Cambridge IGCSE and O Level Global Perspectives syllabus. What do they mean to you?

- globalisation
- values
- inequality

Write down a definition for each of the three words. Now share your definitions with a partner. Do they have the same ideas as you? Finally, look at the definitions for these words given in the glossary. Are they different from yours and your partner's?

ACTIVITY 1.03

You are going to carry out a survey with your class, so that you can all get to know each other a little more.

1   Think of a question that everyone could answer. For example, this could be 'Which is your favourite subject at school?' or 'Where do you feel the happiest?' Make sure it is a question you would be happy to answer. Be ready to share the question you have thought of.

2   Share your question with another person and feed back your questions as a pair to the rest of your class.

3   As a class, collect together everyone's questions and decide which ones you would like to include in the class survey.

4   Write down the questions on a sheet of paper and ask your partner for their answers. Your partner will write down your answers.

5   In a group, compare all your answers and be ready to tell the class about your group. You might choose one reporter to speak for all of you, or you might choose to give your own answers.

6   Hold a class discussion about the similarities and differences in the people in your class. For example, some of you may have the same favourite colour, or school subject, or you may have different ones. Some of your most interesting similarities and differences might be your feelings about things, for example whether the same thing makes you feel happy.

As you have seen, you may feel differently and have different ideas and **values** (beliefs about what is good or correct) from other people. Understanding these differences helps us to understand what a perspective is. Our own personal perspective is based on what we have learned from others, what we have seen and done in our life and what our experiences have been. We also have different ideas because we have different influences. People see the world differently because they think in different ways. Our views are influenced by many people, including our parents, friends and people we admire.

> **KEY TERM**
>
> **values:** moral principles/ideas/ beliefs/feelings about what is morally correct, right, good or desirable.

Perspectives on behaviour

Different groups of people and different cultures have different ideas of what is polite behaviour and what is impolite behaviour. For example, in many European countries, it is considered polite to give a tip/gratuity in a restaurant, particularly if you received good service (often adding around 10% to the bill). In Japan or South Korea, however, offering a tip may be considered rude. In some countries, it is always impolite not to remove your shoes before entering someone's house. However, in other countries, it is expected that you would ask the person whose house you were visiting whether you should take them off; or you might even just be expected to leave them on.

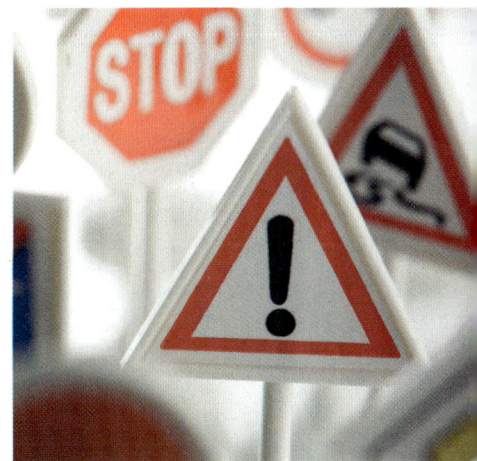

Figure 1.3: Rules help us understand what we need to do

ACTIVITY 1.04

1   List at least two or three examples of behaviours which are considered to be polite in your own country, but rude in other countries; or behaviour which is thought to be rude in your country but polite elsewhere. If you are working in a group, share your examples and make a longer list.

2   Discuss why certain behaviour is considered to be good and other behaviour is considered to be bad.

   a   Are there different rules for children and adults?

   b   Are there different rules for children of different ages? Why is this so?

   c   Why might there be different rules depending on where in the world you live?

   d   Why do we have rules?

3   Create a document called 'Rules of politeness' which displays your findings.

Here is another example of how perspectives about everyday life can differ. Some people like eating meat and think it is ok to do so; other people prefer not to eat meat and may feel that other people should not eat it either. They may have strong views on the subject.

Figure 1.4: People may have different perspectives on whether we should eat meat

Why do you think people have these different perspectives about eating meat? Where might these ideas have come from?

Global, national, local and personal perspectives

In your work on this course you will explore and analyse global, national, local and personal perspectives on a range of global problems, or issues.

A global perspective is a view of the whole world/the planet. This view goes wider than you, your community and the country where you are living. Global issues, such as economic or social issues, are often in the news. A global issue or problem usually needs a global solution. It is not really possible to solve climate change with a local solution.

However, local courses of action might help towards a global solution. For example, a local course of action might be a poster campaign aimed at businesses, encouraging them to reduce the amount of fossil fuels they are using. This is because 'every little helps': if we all do something to change our behaviour, this can have big effects. Other global issues can also be local issues: poverty, for example. In these cases, it might be possible to do something locally. We might be able to take some action to help solve the problem of local poverty, even though we cannot do very much to help on a global scale.

KEY TERMS

global perspective: a perspective about the whole world, or planet Earth.

national perspective: a perspective about a particular country, or common to a whole country (these could be a view of the country given by one person, or a common view of many people in the country).

local perspective: perspective about a local area or the views of a local community.

personal perspective: someone's own view about an issue, usually how it affects them personally.

issue: an important subject or problem for discussion.

economic: about money.

social: about people/society.

solution: a means of solving a problem or dealing with a difficult situation.

course of action: a plan or method used for achieving a specific aim or goal.

ACTIVITY 1.05

1   Look at Figure 1.5. It shows a diamond nine grid which ranks some of the global issues that the world is currently facing. The most important one from this person's perspective is unemployment, which is at the top. Of equal importance underneath are population growth and disease. The issue this person thinks is the least important is at the bottom (crime).

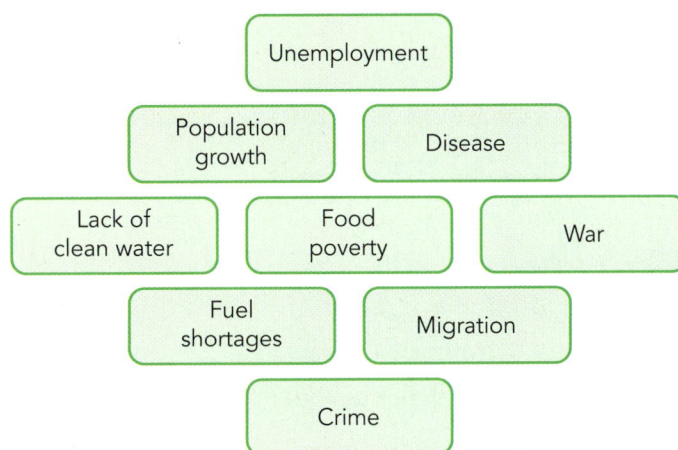

Figure 1.5: Diamond nine grid 'Prioritising global issues'

2   Do you agree with the priorities in the diamond nine grid?

3   Consider which of these you think will be the most important for you over the next twenty years of your life. How might you change the grid (the order of priority, change of issues)?

4   Draw your own diamond nine grid with your own priorities in it.

5   Discuss with your partner the changes you have made to the diagram.

Listen to your partner's perspective. Do you have the same priorities? Why do you think this might be?

You may have a similar perspective and similar priorities as you have some things in common; you are probably the same age, you may have the same friends. You may have a similar family background. You will also have the same influences in school. If you did this activity with someone in a different country or a different type of school, you might find more differences.

1.2 Thinking about topics

In Cambridge IGCSE and O Level Global Perspectives you will not have to know lots of information about topics. Instead, you will research and explore some topics and you will read about, write about and discuss different topics. You will be using these topics to develop your skills and not to learn information for examinations.

You will get the chance to choose topics you are interested in or topics that you do not know much about but you think you would be interested in learning more about.

ACTIVITY 1.06

1   Take a few minutes to think of three important world problems you have heard about, or that you know about. Write them down.

2   For each problem in your list, write down the answers to these questions. Be ready to share your ideas in a group:

   a   Why is this a problem?

   b   Are a lot of people affected by this problem?

   c   How do you know about the problem/where did you find out about it?

   d   Write down two details about the problem.

3   In your group, take it in turns to tell each other about the problems you thought of.

   You may find that some of you came up with some of the same ideas.

4   As a team, design a poster that shows one or two of the problems you thought of and some interesting or important information about each problem. Your poster should be clear and well organised so that anyone looking at it can easily see your ideas.

   a   Decide together how you will organise everything on the poster – you might like to make a small rough draft on a piece of paper.

   b   When you have agreed, decide whether you are all going to put your own ideas on the poster or whether one or two of you should make the poster and put everyone's ideas down on it for them.

   c   Make the poster and then display it for the rest of the class to see.

5   When everyone's posters are ready, do a 'gallery walk': go round and look at the different posters and their ideas. Compare any similarities and differences.

6   Discuss this activity as a class. You should identify the different problems on each of the posters and discuss why these were chosen. You should also talk about the information that has been provided about each problem on the posters. Is it useful? Could it be more detailed? Would this information be helpful to use in finding a solution to the problem? Finally, discuss how the information has been presented on each poster. Could this have been improved? Which poster is best at communicating the problem it has chosen?

As a student of Cambridge Global Perspectives you will explore a number of different topics as you learn and develop skills. Engaging with the topics will help you to improve these skills. You will also choose topics to focus on when you do specific tasks, either on your own or as part of a group. This might involve finding the best match between what you are interested in and one of the topics. For example, if you are interested in the environment, then Climate change, energy and resources; Environment, pollution and conservation; or Water, food and agriculture might all be relevant. If you are interested in art you may choose 'Arts in society', and so on for other topics.

Figure 1.6: Arts in society is one of the topics you can explore

ACTIVITY 1.07

1 Review the list of Cambridge IGCSE and O Level Global Perspectives topics set out in the Introduction.

2 If you are working in a group, discuss what sorts of hobbies, subjects and topics you are interested in.

3 Select the six interests that are most popular in your group.

4 Compare your list of six interests with the list of Cambridge IGCSE and O Level Global Perspectives topics. Choose two or three topics which you think will cover your interests and write them down.

5 As a group, discuss how you could let the rest of the class know the topics you have chosen and the interests that were linked to them. You can make a poster, or you can choose one or two people to be spokespeople to tell the rest of the class about your group's interests and ideas. Or you can choose any other way to tell the class.

6 Share your thoughts with the class.

7 Take a class vote on which topics you like best.

1.3 Thinking about issues

You will have noticed that the Cambridge IGCSE and O Level Global Perspectives topics are very broad headings. 'Health and wellbeing', for example, can cover a lot of different possibilities! This means that you will need to narrow them down to identify the specific problem or point of disagreement you are interested in within the overall topic. In Cambridge Global Perspectives, we call these problems or subjects that people disagree about 'issues'. Issues can cause difficulties for people, or disagreements or even conflicts between different groups or countries. For example, inequality is a global issue.

In Activity 1.07, you matched up things you were interested in with Cambridge IGCSE and O Level Global Perspectives topics. To do this, you needed to match the topics with your interests by breaking down each one to look for points of similarity between them.

Figure 1.7: Inequality is a global issue

ACTIVITY 1.08

With a partner:

1 Look at the posters you created for Activity 1.06 to remind yourselves about them.

2 Choose any one of the posters; it can be a poster created by a different group.

3 Make a note of the world problems on the poster you have chosen.

4 Are there any links between the topics and the problems?

CONTINUED

5   Take a piece of paper and write both your names at the top.

    a   If you can see a topic that links to some of the problems on the poster, write it down on your piece of paper with the title: Topic.

    b   Below it, write 'Issues' as a heading and list three problems that link to the topic, like this:

Jack and Jill

Topic:

Health and wellbeing

Issues:

Vaccination

Childhood diseases

Exercise

6   Now exchange your paper with another pair.

7   Look at what they have written and add any more ideas from any of the other posters.

8   Exchange with a different pair and do the same thing.

9   Then return the paper you have to the people whose names are at the top.

10   When you get your paper back, take a look at what has been added and see if you agree with it.

When you are reading about an issue that people disagree on, you should try to find out what different people think about the issue and why they have different ideas. In other words, you should identify different people's perspectives. When you have heard, or read, both sides of the story you can make up your own mind about what you think. You might agree with one or the other perspective, or you might think both perspectives are understandable but not really agree completely with either one.

Figure 1.8: Working together improves learning outcomes

1.4 Developing skills

The Cambridge IGCSE and O Level Global Perspectives course is all about developing skills that will be useful in your education, work and life repeated below.

Figure 1.9: Cambridge Global Perspectives skills

Look at Figure 1.9. Some of the words might be new or unfamiliar.

Look at the key terms for an explanation of each skill.

You have probably practised these skills in your own life, without thinking about it. This course will help you to develop the skills and make you more aware of your own skills and how you can use them.

ACTIVITY 1.09

Reflect on (think about) the course so far and the activities you have done.

1   In your group, divide up the Cambridge Global Perspectives skills. Each one of you should think about one skill. Write the name of your skill on a piece of paper.

2   Think about the activities you have done that can relate to that skill – if you feel you have not done any related activities, has anyone else in the class done any? One of your classmates, the teacher? If you are not sure, discuss with a partner. Write down the activities on your skill paper. You can list them or write them in around the skill name.

3   Share what you have written with the rest of your group. Do they have any other ideas?

4   Listen to the others' ideas and suggest any others you can think of.

5   As a group, join another group and compare your skills papers.

KEY TERMS

analysis: studying or examining the parts of something, or the details, to understand it better.

collaboration: working together with others in a supportive and effective way.

communication: sharing ideas, feelings or information with others by speaking, in writing or in any other way.

evaluation: working out if something is useful, valuable, effective, by looking at its good points and its bad points, or its strengths and weaknesses.

reflection: thinking deeply. This could be about something that has happened, something you have learned, or how to get your own ideas and feelings clear in your own mind.

research: the systematic study of a global issue to find evidence and develop understanding.

REFLECTION

Look back at your self-evaluation at the beginning of the chapter. Do any of the ratings need to change? Is there anything you would like to add that you feel you understand better?

SHOWCASING YOUR SKILLS

Cambridge Global Perspectives

Your class is going to start its own Cambridge Global Perspectives magazine or newsletter.

Take a few moments to think about any newsletters or magazines you have seen. How would you describe a magazine to someone who had never seen one? Note down three elements you might find in a magazine or newsletter.

Share your ideas with others in your class. Which of these ideas do you think you could include in your class magazine or newsletter? You will now need to make sure you include the different parts that a newsletter or magazine will need. What is the most important story about global perspectives which you want to headline on, or make your cover story? What sections will your publication have? And who will be responsible for each section, or for writing the headlines?

Your first edition will be a general introduction to Cambridge Global Perspectives and to your classmates. Everyone in the class will be involved.

You can add new editions later in the course, with contributions from the class on different experiences of your course, class and the topics and issues you cover during the course.

Reflection on your showcase

Write a few lines describing what went well.

Was the first draft of the magazine/newsletter successful? How do you know?

What was difficult?

How could you improve things for next time?

Did you enjoy preparing the magazine?

Did this activity help you to think about what you had learned in Chapter 1?

SUMMARY

In Chapter 1 you have been thinking about Cambridge Global Perspectives and practising pair work and group work.

You have considered different people's perspectives and thought about global, national, local and personal perspectives.

You have looked at some topics that you will be examining and skills you will be developing during the course. You have considered world problems and issues you know about.

You have collaborated with others and discussed how activities can develop the skills and you have been involved in starting a Cambridge Global Perspectives magazine or newsletter.

REVIEW AND REFLECTION

	I have learned about ...	I need more practice with ...
Perspectives, including global, national, local and personal perspectives		
Topics and issues		
Skills developed in Cambridge Global Perspectives		

Active learning

In this chapter, you will start by learning about how your brain works. This will help you to explore a number of different ways in which you can improve your memory in general, as well as choosing the best method to stay focused on your work. Because the brain works by making and storing connections, you can support your memory by using effective strategies to connect with your learning, and this chapter explores a range of techniques for doing this. After that, it discusses reflection, specifically how to reflect on your learning. Finally, you will consider how you can learn effectively from other people and the different ways in which this happens as you work as a team.

This chapter uses examples from the topics of Migration and urbanisation, Climate change, energy and resources, Environment, pollution and conservation, Employment, and Globalisation to explore and develop skills of active learning.

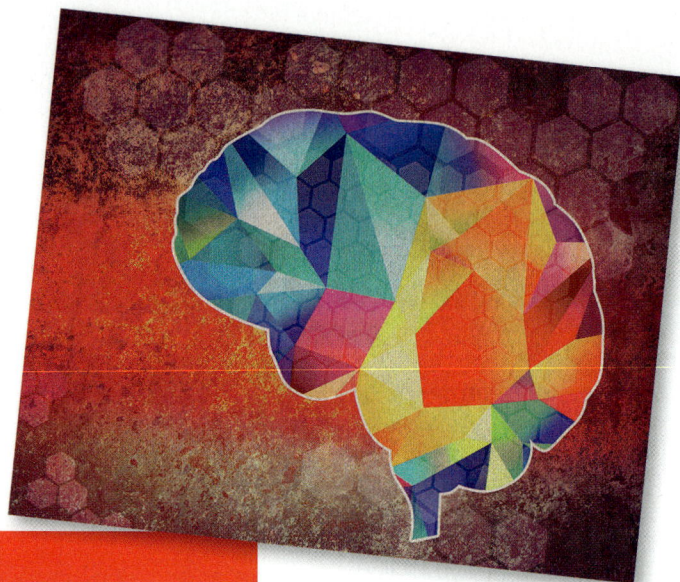

BEFORE YOU START

Before you start work on this chapter, take a few minutes to think about the things you do independently now and how you learned to do them. How do you remember important things? Write down your ideas.

2.1 Memory and learning skills

In this section, we will learn about how the memory works and how we can improve our memory and learn more easily by using organisational tools and **metacognition** strategies. We need to use memory effectively in order to store information and skills. Scientists are now beginning to recognise that anyone can learn at any time in their life. To allow you to do that, you may need to change the way you do things so that you can remember better.

KEY TERM

metacognition: thinking about learning more explicitly, often by selecting a suitable strategy for planning, monitoring or evaluation of learning.

REFLECTION

Think about how you have learned to do things in your everyday life.

- Do you have a good memory?

- Do you remember some types of information easily but find others more difficult to remember?

- What sorts of things do you find easy to remember?

- How do you remember specific information, for example tests and exams, or directions to a specific place?

Discuss your thoughts with a partner.

How our brain works

Our brain helps us to take in important information and remember it for future use. The brain works as a filter, keeping important information and experiences in our long-term memory for us to access later. It filters out things that are not so important. This often happens without us noticing.

The brain puts everything into our short-term memory first and then filters what we hear and see so we can concentrate on what is important. This means that we can listen to one person when there are other people talking. But we can be distracted by a sudden loud noise. The brain also filters what we see so that we notice the things that are important for our survival.

If we want to remember information and experiences, we have to make sure the brain keeps them stored for us. An example of this is learning the alphabet, or the multiplication tables. Our long-term memory helps us to build on our learning from before, without having to start at the beginning. To help us to do this, we can use a range of strategies and techniques to ensure that the information we need can be accessed easily when we need it.

The more we learn, the better we get at learning. It is a bit like exercise; the more we do, the fitter we get. Changing the way you do things, including how you learn, is what this section on memory is about.

Figure 2.1: The wonderful human brain

Making connections

All our knowledge is connected together like a spider's web. Learning new concepts and ideas happens easily when we already have some knowledge about what we are learning. However, we find learning harder when we have fewer connections to the subject we are trying to learn. Making connections not only helps us to learn but also helps us to remember the information we have learned so we can use it again in the future.

Making these connections with our learning takes time and practice, just like learning to play a sport. In physical activities, we build up skills that help us to be better at future physical activities. Sometimes we need to connect what we are doing to things we have done before and use our knowledge or skills to help us to do new things. The same is true of new ideas. When we learn something new, we need to make connections; we link ideas and information together, or we link to things we already know in a different way that increases our ability to make new connections. We need to associate new ideas and information with each other and with the ones we already have.

ACTIVITY 2.01

Look at the diagram below. Copy out the diagram and add your own connections or associations. As a challenge, why not try creating a real life version of this diagram by finding connections between other learners. For example you could try finding connections between birthdays or try something harder like foods people like/dislike or hobbies.

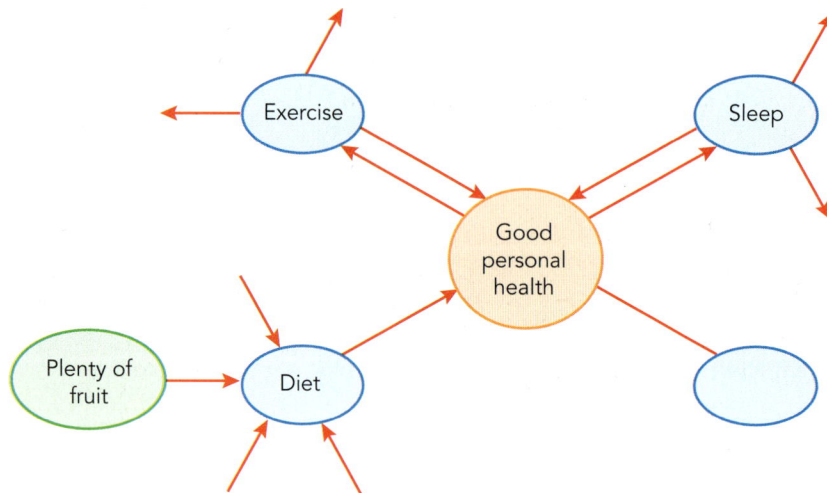

Figure 2.2: Making connections

Mind-maps

One good way to link ideas and record connections is to use a mind-map. Mind-maps organise information visually around a single idea or issue. Brief and clear supporting points, words or examples are written down and linked to the key issue using lines to show the connection, sometimes emphasising the most important supporting information.

Mind-maps are a useful tool to use when there is a lot of information to consider or when the links between ideas are hard to see. Mind-maps allow these supporting ideas to link to each other and can use colours and pictures to show connections to the central theme or issue, as in Figure 2.3.

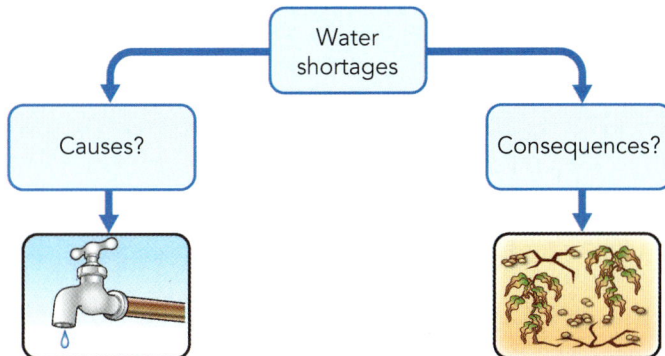

Figure 2.3: Example of a mind-map

Advantages

- Mind-maps can use words and images and are often colourful.

- Mind-maps help you to record what you already know about a topic or issue, and allow you to connect prior learning to new learning.

- Mind-maps allow you to add words and images connected to the key idea or issue, or any branches off that key idea or issue.

Spidergrams

A spider diagram or spidergram is a form of mind-map which uses lines and circles to make connections (Figure 2.4). It is particularly helpful for organising information into different topics.

A spidergram starts with a central idea and branches out. You should use a whole sheet of A4 paper and put the main idea in the centre. You can then draw branches pointing outwards. You should use one branch per point. By adding smaller branches, you can add detail and examples. This is a useful tool to use when planning writing as the supporting information you include on the branches can show you if your ideas group together in a **logical** way, and whether your points have enough supporting detail or examples.

> **KEY TERM**
>
> **logical:** sensible and reasonable.

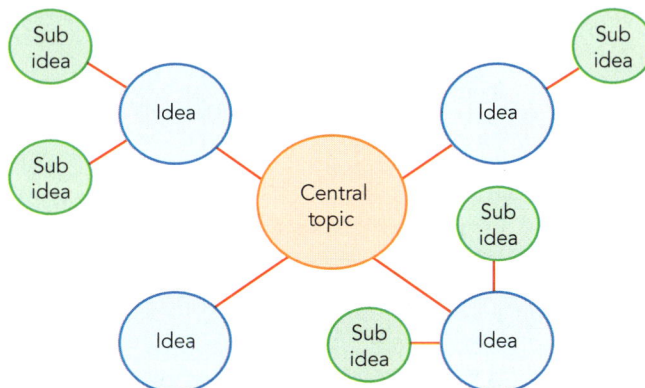

Figure 2.4: Example of a spidergram

Advantages

- All your notes are on one page, so you are less likely to write irrelevant information.

- You can see the main points straightaway.

- You can connect key points and ideas, which is good for structuring a report or essay.

- You can clearly see where there are gaps where you need to do more research.

ACTIVITY 2.02

Explore the use of spidergrams by putting the word 'spidergrams' into your search engine. Save or print two examples that you think might help you use this technique in the future.

ACTIVITY 2.03

Read this text on the global topic of Employment, then do the activity below.

> Getting paid for working in a job is one of the best ways to get out of poverty. Good jobs play a vital role in giving people a sense of wellbeing and confidence. Having a job makes a person feel as if they are making a contribution to their family and their community.
>
> However, unemployment is rising across the world and is becoming a serious global issue. There have already been protests and uprisings in places like Brazil and Greece because people are not able to earn a living to feed themselves or their families. Another effect of unemployment is the increased population within towns and cities as people move from the countryside to where the work is. Overpopulation leads to overcrowding and poor-quality housing in many large cities. Poorly heated or damp housing can cause serious health issues, resulting in illnesses such as pneumonia. Another serious consequence of overcrowding is rising crime, as poor living conditions can lead some people to make desperate choices and break the law.
>
> '*The more people are employed, the better the living standards and the healthier and happier the community*', states Henry Gold from the World Bank.

Produce a spidergram of the key points. You do not need to record everything in your diagram. You might find it easier to write some headings after reading the text once, for example:

- benefits of a job

- effects of unemployment

- consequences of rural unemployment

- consequences of overpopulated towns.

Organising information

You will remember more if you are organised. Our brains like order and can make connections more quickly if the information it is given is organised. It is why planning is an essential skill for the Cambridge IGCSE and O Level Global Perspectives course. An example of organising would be that this text book is set out with chapters, sections and headings so that you can easily follow the flow of information and your brain will understand it more quickly and remember it better.

ACTIVITY 2.04

Look at the lists below. Who do you think might have written them?
Why did they write them and how will they use these lists?

1 kilo rice 2 kilo onions Garlic Tomatoes Oil Flour Chocolate	*On my way home:* *Pick up Jack & Nabil from school* *Post parcel* *Drop Jack off at the swimming pool* *Collect books from Rekha before 5*	Homework Geog - revise chapter 6 - open book test Mon. Maths - worksheet finding the median. 1st 10. Eng - Read passage page 27 and answer Q 1-4.

Write down your thoughts and share them with a partner.

Timelines

Timelines are a useful way of organising notes to make sense of when things happen.

In Figure 2.5, the timeline shows some of the significant events to do with plastic production and pollution from 1839 to 2021.

1839	1839	1856	1872	1926
Natural Rubber Method of processing invented by Charles Goodyear	**Polystyrene (PS)** Discovered by Eduard Simon	**Parkesine** Invented by Alexander Parkes	**Polyvinyl Chloride (PVC)** First created by Eugen Baumann	**Vinyl or PVC** Plasticised PVC invented by Waldo Semon

1951	1941	1941	1936	1935
High-density Polyethylene (HDPE) Invented by Paul Hogan and Robert Banks	**Polyethylene Terephthalate (PET)** Invented by Whinfield and Dickson	**Styrofoam** Invented by Ray McIntire for Dow Chemical	**Acrylic** Poly Methyl Methacrylate Invented by Hill and Crawford	**Low-density Polyethylene (LDPE)** Invented by Reginald Gibson and Eric Fawcett

1951	1960	1997	2021
Polypropylene (PP) Also invented by Paul Hogan and Robert Banks	**Plastic Pollution** First observed in the ocean. First plastic bag off the coast of Ireland.	**Garbage Patch** Great Pacific Garbage Patch discovered by Charles Moore	**Actions to Mitigate** Global Plastic Standards, Regulations, Protests and NGOs fight to reduce plastic

Figure 2.5: Timeline of plastic production and pollution, 1839–2021

Advantages

- A timeline gives you a visual image of a series of important events in date order.

- You can use a timeline to make notes about an issue and how it happened, for example the spread of COVID-19 in 2020. Search for 'COVID-19 pandemic timeline' to see some examples.

- You can easily add events to a timeline, so they are useful for planning projects.

Flow charts

A flow chart is a diagram that can be used to represent a process. The steps are shown in boxes and are connected with arrows, as shown in Figure 2.6.

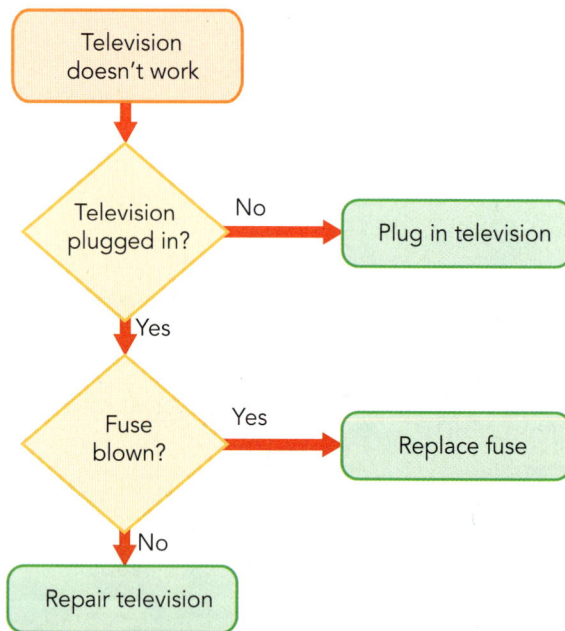

Figure 2.6: Example of a flow chart

Advantages

- Flow charts help you to gain an idea of the steps you need to take to complete something, for example a research task or a project.

- You can easily add in information as you think of further steps in the process.

Planning

Organising information is often followed by consolidating it and turning it into your own piece of work, for example a written report or essay, a visual presentation, or a basis for a course of action. When completing any piece of work, you should get into the habit of following the steps shown in Figure 2.7.

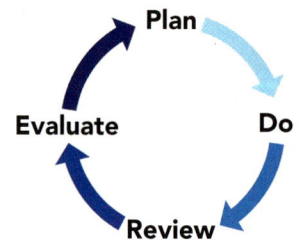

Figure 2.7: Steps for completing a piece of work

Planning is a skill you will use throughout your life. It requires practice, as do all the skills within this book.

When creating a plan, you should always try to create a **SMART plan**. SMART stands for:

Specific

Measurable

Achievable

Relevant

Timely

You should be able to answer the following questions to create a SMART plan:

1 **Specific** – What are you trying to achieve? How are you going to achieve it?

2 **Measurable** – How will you assess whether you have achieved what you set out to achieve? How will you know when you have finished it?

3 **Achievable** – Do you have the skills and resources to achieve your aim? If not, can you access them?

4 **Relevant** – Is this what is required? Will it match requirements?

5 **Timely** – What is your time frame? Can you achieve this in the time? (If not, you will need to change the time frame or your plan.)

ACTIVITY 2.05

Consider the following long-term goal: To cook a special meal for a family member's birthday.

1 Identify four short-term goals to reach your long-term goal.

2 Discuss your short-term goals with a partner. Do they have the same ideas as you?

Short-term goals might include: find or ask someone for a recipe, buy the ingredients, set a date and time, enlist a friend to help.

3 Write a reflection: Why is it so useful to break down your plan into smaller short-term goals? Could you use this technique for your longer-term life goals? Think of some examples.

Using metacognition

In order to be more effective in our learning, we can consciously decide how we plan, monitor or **evaluate** our learning. This is called metacognition. When we use metacognition, we are making important decisions about how we use this stored information to learn. Being aware of what strategies and tools are useful to the task helps you to learn more effectively, as you will be able to manage lots of information and evaluate what is important and what is not.

ACTIVITY 2.06

Think about things you can do, either well or badly, or subjects you know a lot about.

Create a table like the one below. In the left-hand Activity column, make a short list of these things. These can be everyday activities you do, sports, games you play, hobbies, skills you have learned such as reading and writing, knowledge you have about hobbies, your interests or your studies.

Activity	Could I do it without practice?	How long I have spent doing it?	What did/would I do to improve my skill?

Now look at your list of the things you do well: did you have to practise them before you became good at them? Did you know how to do them perfectly the first time? How much time have you spent doing them? What skills did you already have that helped you to learn to sing, play a musical instrument, play sports, hobbies or games? If you haven't ever learned to play an instrument, do you think it would take a long time to play well? Make notes in your table.

With a partner, share your thoughts and experiences and then decide between you: is it possible to learn something new without practising? Find some examples to support your answer to this question.

Techniques to help your learning

Pictures and images help us to remember things for longer. This is because they often connect to something we already know and can compress complex ideas into something simpler that sticks in our minds. Try drawing little pictures or cartoons, or look online for pictures, to help you remember key ideas and issues (Figure 2.8).

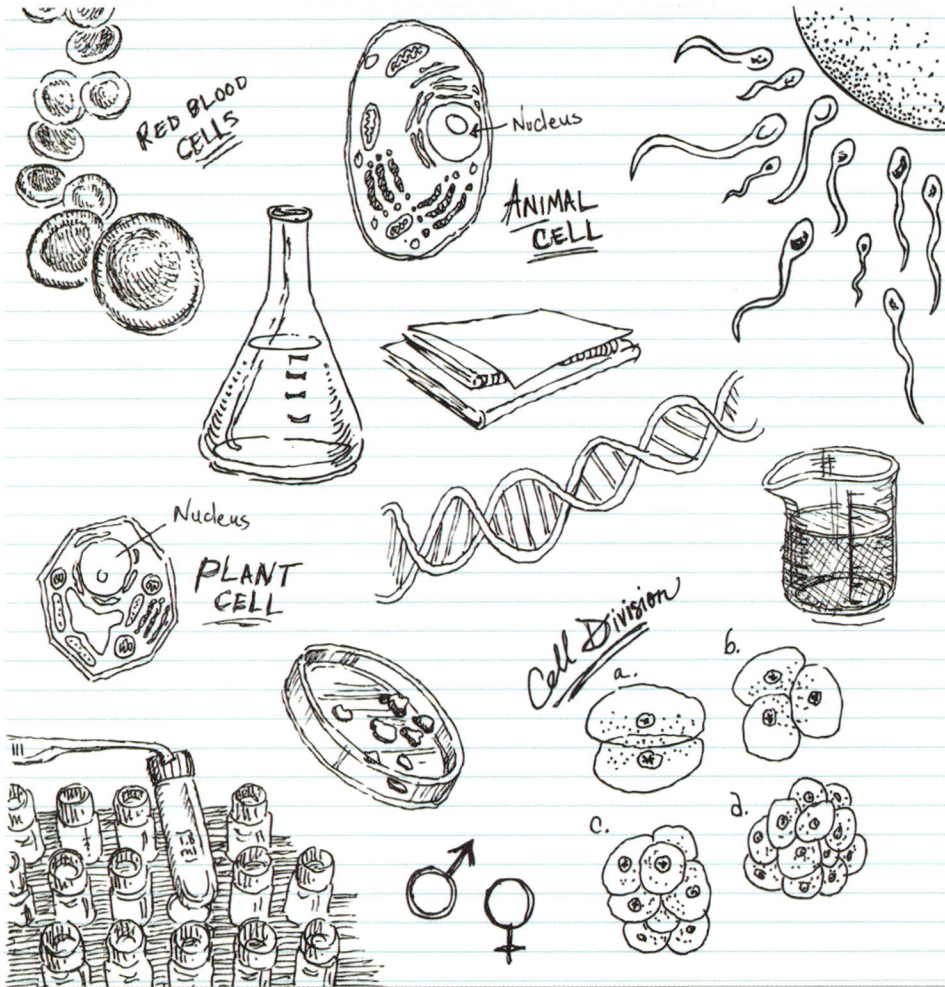

Figure 2.8: Drawing pictures can help you remember details

ACTIVITY 2.07

1   Search the internet to find an image to help you remember how the brain makes connections.

2   Find an image that sums up an issue to do with the Cambridge IGCSE and O Level Global Perspectives topic of Migration and urbanisation. Consider these questions:

   a   What issues does the picture represent?

   b   If you see this picture in the future, will you remember the issue(s)?

CONTINUED

3   When looking at Figure 2.9, what issue(s) do you think of?

Figure 2.9: A city skyline

When looking at Figure 2.9, it is likely that you thought of burning fossil fuels and how the world's use of resources, especially energy, causes climate change. You might also have considered the **globalisation** of humanity's energy needs and the global impact they have. The impact of pollution on the environment through industrial activity is also something this picture might get you thinking about. All of these are relevant global issues to consider when studying Cambridge Global Perspectives and are linked to the Cambridge IGCSE and O Level Global Perspectives topics.

Another idea to help you learn is to simplify information into an **acronym** to help you remember key features or ideas. For example, to remind yourself what to edit in your writing you might use the acronym 'GAPS':

G   grammar

A   accurate punctuation

P   paragraphs

S   spelling

KEY TERMS

globalisation: the development of close connections between all (or most) of the countries in the world, building closer economic, cultural, and political relations between them. This is happening because communication and travel are easier now.

acronym: an abbreviation formed from the initial letters of other words and pronounced as a word.

Figure 2.10: Acronyms simplify information and help us to remember

Keeping focused

When learning, it is important to focus on the task in hand. This gives your brain time to move what you are learning from your short-term memory, where it might be forgotten, into your long-term memory so that you can remember it. Multi-tasking can prevent you from doing this.

Spending longer at your computer will not help you remember more. Even an adult can only concentrate for a maximum of fifteen to twenty minutes at any one time, so have a break when you need to. Getting up and doing something different for a couple of minutes will help you to refocus when you return to your work. Physical activity not only helps keep your body fit but also helps keep your brain fit and aids memory.

The **Pomodoro technique** is a popular method for keeping focused on one task at a time; it helps you stay focused by prompting you to take breaks when you need to. It uses a timer to measure out intervals of work on one task (usually lasting about twenty minutes) with breaks of five minutes built in between intervals. The breaks are designed to make it easier to return to single-minded attention on the task. This technique was invented by Francesco Cirillo in the late 1980s who used a kitchen timer in the shape of a tomato ('pomodoro' means tomato in Italian). Today, you can either use a mechanical or electronic timer, or there are many phone and computer apps available which provide a Pomodoro timer.

> **KEY TERM**
>
> **Pomodoro technique:** a method for timing work in set intervals with built-in breaks.

> **REFLECTION**
>
> Think about the different methods for improving your memory and learning that we have looked at in this section. Do you know any other methods that would be helpful? Which of these methods do you think will help you personally in the future?

2.2 The skill of reflection

Reflection means thinking about something in depth. We can reflect on things we are going to do, to prepare or plan, or we can reflect on things after they have happened. Reflection is a key part of metacognition.

Reflection is helpful in learning because it helps us to remember and learn from our experiences or our studies. Sometimes we need to reflect on things to understand them better.

Reflection is one of the skills you will learn and practise in Cambridge Global Perspectives:

- When responding to written questions, you will need to use your reflection skills and also be prepared to give your own view.

- When working on an individual report, you will reflect on your research findings and the different perspectives you have explored; you will give your own perspective on the issue you have researched, explaining how your perspective has been affected by your research.

- After you have completed a team project, you will reflect on your experiences, what you found out and how the project went – the successes and struggles.

Throughout this book, you will be given opportunities to think about your own ideas and beliefs and learning.

REFLECTION

Think about reflection. In your daily life, when do you find yourself reflecting on what has happened in your life or things you have done? Why do you do this? Is it because you want to relive moments you enjoyed? Do you think of how things could have been different and how you could have changed them?

Share your thoughts with your partner. Does your partner reflect on the same things? Do they reflect in the same way? Do you both spend time reflecting?

Reflection for learning

Ask yourself the following question: Am I already a reflective learner?

If the answer is yes, then well done, but keep reading as you can always get better at reflection. If the answer is no, then don't worry. This section gives you some activities and tips to help you on your way to becoming a more reflective learner.

Being able to reflect will improve your learning, so you need to find time to do it. Reflecting on the learning you do in the classroom can help you identify areas that you could improve on. It can also help you to think of next steps and plan different ways of doing an activity or project. You might say that you are always thinking anyway, but it is not enough just to think; you have to communicate your thoughts to someone else.

So, although reflection itself is an independent activity, you will improve your learning if you share your reflections, either in written or spoken form. The easiest option is to write down your reflections. You can keep a diary, keeping your thoughts private, or write a blog and share your thoughts with others.

Figure 2.11: Am I already a reflective learner?

Thinking about the reflection tasks you've already completed, you'll notice that you reflected on what you already knew, looking back to the past and making connections to your prior knowledge. In Activity 2.01, you were able to add your thoughts to the 'Making connections' diagram in Figure 2.2, showing your knowledge. Then in Activity 2.06 you reflected on things you can do and what you need to do to improve, using metacognition. So you can reflect looking back: thinking about what has happened or what you have done. Or you can reflect looking ahead: planning or thinking about what you want to do or are hoping to do.

When you use a strategy such as mind-mapping, timelines or flow charts, you have to select what you want to write down. You reflect to select. Then you need to use the information given carefully: read it and reflect on it, then decide what is important and can be used.

When you want to revise material for other subjects, these strategies will help you to think back to what you have learned, or to the advice your teacher has given you.

> **DISCUSSION**
>
> With a partner, discuss how reflecting in this way helps you to learn and how it links to what you have learned about memory skills.

> **REFLECTION**
>
> Think about: What learning strategies help you to remember what you have learned? Note down your thoughts.

2.3 Sharing ideas and working as a team

Think about sharing ideas: Why is it important to share our ideas when we work or play with other people? What happens if we do not share ideas?

If we share ideas when we are with other people, they know what we are thinking and can take our feelings or ideas into consideration. If we do not tell people what we think, they have no way of understanding us. It is easier to work with other people if we cooperate and work as a team. This includes sharing our own knowledge and ideas. There may be more than one possible way of doing something; sharing different ideas helps us to come up with the best solution.

Figure 2.12: Working as a team can improve knowledge

Sharing our own ideas and discussing them with others can make them clearer to us. Sometimes saying our ideas out loud helps us to see them clearly. Discussing and sharing our thoughts can help us to get them clear in our minds. Sometimes we only realise if our ideas are good or not when we tell someone else.

REFLECTION

What do you speak about to your family and friends? Why do you talk to them about these things?

When you share your ideas with others, what makes it easy or difficult to do this? How can you get your ideas clear before you share them?

When you work in a team, you have to share ideas and information (Figure 2.12). You have to divide the workload so that everyone has a role and is included. You have to support others and work as a team successfully. This means understanding how others feel and thinking about everyone's strengths and weaknesses so that you can complete your work in good time.

ACTIVITY 2.08

Take time to think of a problem that you think needs to be solved at your school or in your local area. Get your ideas clear in your own mind – you may like to do some research or just note down your ideas as you will be sharing them in your group. Choose only one idea to share, but don't forget your other thoughts in case you need to change your mind. Be ready to explain why you think this is a problem that needs to be solved.

Decide how you will share your ideas with your group and get ready to do so. You could do this formally, for example by giving a presentation or sharing a handout or a leaflet, or informally by chatting together in your group.

TIP

When working as a team to research a topic and/or issue, you all have to discuss and agree a topic and an issue to work on. You do some individual research. Then you share your findings with the rest of the group. This helps you to decide on what you will do as a group. You have to divide the workload and find a way of making a difference as a group.

You will learn more about teamwork in Chapter 7 Collaboration.

Listening attentively

We often learn information and ideas by hearing them from teachers, parents and friends. Sometimes we might hear the expression 'in one ear and out the other'. That is used when someone says something, and we immediately forget it! In this section, you are going to practise listening carefully in group activities.

Think about listening. Why are listening skills helpful in learning and in your life in general? What happens if you do not listen carefully to others?

Figure 2.13: Listening is an important skill

ACTIVITY 2.09

When you work in a team or in a group, it is good to have some ground rules to make sure that everyone is included and feels comfortable. Some people find it easy to talk in groups and others tend to be quieter.

But to work properly together, you have to make sure that everyone takes part in discussions and that everyone knows what is happening. In your group, discuss how you will make sure that when you work together in future, everyone is heard and that everyone listens to what the others have to say. Use some of the memory skills ideas to make sure you remember who said what.

Share your ideas from Activity 2.08 with your group. Are there any similarities or differences between your ideas and those of others? Discuss these with your group.

What would you have to do to agree on choosing one of these problems for a team project? Would you discuss it? How would you make sure that everyone was happy with the choice? Would you vote? If so, how would you do that? Raise hands? Say yes or no? Write your answers on slips of paper?

SHOWCASING YOUR SKILLS

Active learning

You will be working with a group on a short project to practise your active learning skills, including teamwork.

As a group, choose a problem or issue that you would like to work on together.

CONTINUED

Your aim is to present your problem, ideas and information to the rest of the class. You might also include a solution to your problem or suggest an alternative.

You can choose to present it as a poster – this could be a flow chart or a mind-map or any other visual aid, or you could give a small presentation, for example as a role play. Your group should not take more than five minutes to present.

You will need to do the following:

1 Individually, create a spidergram of all the things you know about your problem or issue.

2 Compare with your group. What are the similarities? What are the differences? Discuss and decide as a group what you will select to present and why it should be included.

3 Decide if you have enough information or need to do any extra research. Keep the research simple. Do not collect too much extra information.

4 Organise your information as a group. Will it all fit into a five-minute presentation, or will you need to make changes?

5 Divide the work up so that everyone is involved. If you are making a poster, you could all draw or write part of it.

6 Discuss and decide if one of you will do the presenting, or will you organise yourselves as a group to present to the class?

7 Work together to get the poster or presentation ready.

8 Present your team project to the rest of the class.

9 Get some feedback from your class. Did they enjoy your presentation? Could you have done anything differently?

Reflection on your showcase

Write a few lines describing what went well in your work together.

Do you feel you achieved your aim? (Did you do what you planned? Was the presentation successful? What feedback did you get from the class?)

What was difficult? How will you overcome any difficulties for next time?

What have you learned about working in a team?

How could you improve things for next time?

Have you learned something about your topic that you did not know before?

SUMMARY

In Chapter 2, you have been thinking about and practising active learning.

You have looked at some independent learning skills, including ways of improving how you learn, organising your thoughts, and reflection.

You have also thought about and practised working with others. You have shared your ideas and listened attentively to others. You used all these skills to practise working in teams.

REVIEW AND REFLECTION

	I have learned about …	I need more practice with …
How the brain works when remembering information		
Techniques to help me remember and to manage information		
Using metacognition to help me learn		
Techniques to help me learn effectively and stay focused		
The importance of reflection for learning		
Sharing ideas and listening attentively		
Working in a team		

> Chapter 3
Analysis

In this chapter and later in the course, you will learn how to **analyse** sources of information and **arguments**. Analysis is a key skill the study of Cambridge Global Perspectives. When you are analysing an issue or a topic, you will need to consider the causes of the issue and its consequences and think carefully about the arguments you read. This will help you to find suitable arguments and information for the research that you undertake in the course and to have a clearer understanding of how arguments are constructed. It will help you to recognise elements that might show that a text is more or less believable, reliable or plausible.

Analysing texts carefully helps us to notice when the author has provided evidence for their claims, supporting their reasoning and making their argument stronger. Learning the terms we use when we analyse texts will help you to write about others' arguments and perspectives. It will also help you to explore different possible courses of action so that you can choose the best one based on the evidence and reasoning presented. You will also need to analyse arguments when you answer written questions and when you write an individual report or essay. Analysis skills will help you when you consider different perspectives when preparing to write an individual report or when working on a team project.

In this chapter you will be looking at some material on the topics of Water, food and agriculture, Conflict and peace, Education for all, Health and wellbeing, Transport, travel and tourism, Environment, pollution and conservation, Poverty and inequality, and Globalisation. You will learn how to identify different elements of an argument and compare arguments and examine the causes and consequences of issues. At the end of the chapter you will showcase your skills by analysing text and answering questions on it.

KEY TERMS

analyse: to examine something in detail to understand what it is and how it is constructed.

argument: a series of statements containing reasons and evidence which support a claim about a global issue.

REFLECTION

Reflect on your understanding of analysis. What parts did you already know, and what was new information?

BEFORE YOU START

Think about situations where you might need to have a strong argument to make your point. How do you try to support your own arguments? How do you try to prove that what you are saying or writing is true? What proof (evidence) do you use? Do you have to use proof in any of your other subjects? Jot down your thoughts.

3.1 Analysing issues and arguments

To analyse an issue, you need to find out general information about the issue including: **facts**, figures and **opinions** (you will learn more about these in Section 3.3 of this chapter). You must also find out about the causes and consequences of the issue. Understanding causes and consequences helps you to plan possible courses of action or solutions to the issue you are analysing. Some of the questions you could ask include:

- What causes this issue?

- What are the reasons this happens?

- Why do people have this problem?

- What happens to people as a result of the issue?

- What impact does the issue have?

- Does it affect other people/society as a whole?

Understanding the causes and consequences will also help you to better understand the various arguments surrounding your issue. An argument is made up of one or more reasons which try to persuade us to accept a **proposal** or opinion on an issue. Reasons are statements which support the proposal or opinion. When we refer to **reasoning** we are thinking of how strong that support is. If an argument makes sense, the reasoning is considered **sound**. If an argument does not have solid reasons to support the point it is trying to make, or if it uses reasons that do not make sense, it is considered to have unsound reasoning.

We also expect that the reasons in an argument will be supported by **evidence**. Evidence is information or facts which support the reasons, showing that they are true and making us more likely to support them. If the reasons in an argument are supported by evidence, the argument is more likely to be sound.

Evidence can take a variety of forms. For example, it might consist of a photograph, an item of clothing, a table of **statistics** from an official report, a letter or other personal correspondence, or it might be **anecdotal evidence** from someone talking about their experiences.

When using evidence to support your arguments, you should make sure that the evidence is relevant – in other words, that it is directly related to the issue that you are discussing. Evidence is considered 'good' if it can be checked in more than one source. This means that the information contained in the evidence can also be found in other places, written about or spoken by different people. Information that you should check include names, dates, places, events and statistics.

Evidence that cannot be checked in this way may not be relevant or sound. This is particularly important for anecdotes, as it is difficult to check whether the person telling the story was there, and if what they claim actually happened. However, if the story can be backed up by similar anecdotes or evidence from other unrelated sources, then the anecdotal evidence can be considered good and useful to the argument.

You will need to analyse arguments in order to compare them with other arguments, or just to see if they are relevant to your research and whether they are strong and convincing arguments.

KEY TERMS

fact: something that is known or can be proved to be true.

opinion: a personal belief or idea that may or may not be correct.

proposal: something (for example a claim or statement) that is put forward for consideration.

reasoning: thinking in a clear and sensible way. In writing, reasoning means a series of reasons that support an author's perspective or argument.

sound: in the context of a disagreement, an argument that is convincing because it has reasons and evidence that effectively support its conclusions.

evidence: information about a global issue that helps to develop understanding or prove that something is true or false.

statistics: numerical data collected and analysed for the purpose of evidence in support of claims for arguments.

anecdotal evidence: evidence in the form of stories people tell about their experiences.

ACTIVITY 3.01

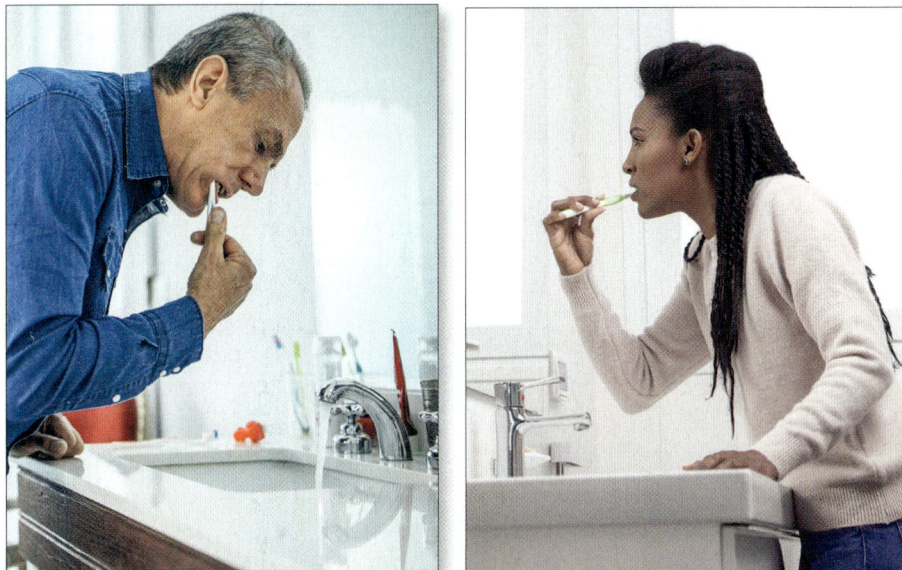

Figure 3.1: Tap running versus tap turned off

1   Read the text about the issue of saving water and answer the questions that follow.

> ### Turn off the water while brushing your teeth
>
> Why should I have to turn off the water while I clean my teeth just because someone says there are water shortages and water should be saved? In the first place, I don't enjoy brushing my teeth, it is not a fun activity! Secondly, it's really annoying that I'm told that I have to turn off the water. Everyone else in my family turns the water off when they brush their teeth, so it shouldn't matter if I do or not, since I'm only one person.

a   How good do you think this argument is?

b   What reasoning is used for the argument?

c   Does the author give any evidence to support the reasoning?

Everything the author says might be true, but it is not a very good argument. It is clear that the author judges that it should not matter if they turn the water off. However, the argument does not answer the point about water shortages. It does not give us any evidence about water shortages.

It is not much more than the author's feelings and their ideas about cleaning their teeth and being told to do something.

CONTINUED

2   Now read another argument about the same issue.

> **Turn off the water while brushing your teeth**
>
> You really should turn off the water when you brush your teeth. Firstly, there is no reason to leave the water running, because when you're brushing your teeth, you're not using the water, so it's simply being wasted. You only need to turn it on first when you wet your toothbrush and then again when you rinse your mouth and your toothbrush.
>
> Another reason to turn off the water when you brush your teeth for two minutes is that you could save eight litres of water every time. The average amount of running water from a tap is five litres of water per minute. If you turn off the water while you are brushing, you will only use two litres. By turning the water off while you brush your teeth, you will help save water in our town, which needs it, because it rains so little here and we have water shortages.

Answer the same three questions:

a   How good do you think this second argument is?

b   What reasoning is used for the argument?

c   Does the author give any evidence to support the reasoning?

3   Now think about causes and consequences relating to the issue and answer the following questions:

a   Why do you think people turn the water off or leave it on?

b   What impacts would happen if people turned off the water to brush their teeth?

c   How would this affect other people/society as a whole?

4   Compare your answers with a partner. Discuss which argument you think is better. Why?

Could the first argument be improved? If so, how? Could the author convince us of their idea that it does not matter what they do if everyone else follows the rules? What consequences would this have?

You should have noticed that the second argument is better. It is not all about feelings and opinions. It has sound reasoning. The writer gives us supporting evidence – the amount of water saved and used in brushing teeth. The evidence is clearly relevant to the issue of saving water as it is about turning the tap off during teeth brushing.

Counter argument

Sometimes **counter argument** is used to introduce an opposing argument or set of ideas. This can deepen your understanding of the argument by giving you evidence and reasoning that presents a different view of the issue.

ACTIVITY 3.02

1   Read the short text below, which relates to the topic of Globalisation, and answer the questions that follow.

> Globalisation has more drawbacks than benefits. This is because in the developing world globalisation has not made the lives of people better and it has failed to reduce poverty. Many people in the developing world are still living on less than one dollar a day. Though the World Poverty Clock (World Data Lab, 2022) reports that poverty is reducing across the world, it also states that over 685 million people are still living in extreme poverty.
>
> Globalisation has increased international trade. This has led to an increase in the number of people employed. This has not been a good thing as in the developing world many employees of large, mostly western, companies work in so-called sweatshops in appalling conditions, which are often dangerous and can be fatal. In July 2021 at least 52 mostly teenage workers died in a sweatshop factory when a blaze engulfed a multi-storey food and beverage factory, just outside Bangladesh's capital of Dhaka.
>
> Additionally, the growth in competition has forced some companies to reduce their workforce so that they can cut costs and increase profits. For example, in countries which have recently experienced strong economic growth, unemployment has started to become a real issue, especially in towns and cities.

a   What do you think the main argument of the text is?

b   How good do you think this argument is?

c   What reasoning is used for the argument?

d   Does the author give any evidence to support the reasoning?

CONTINUED

2   Share your answers to questions **a** to **d** with a partner. When you have done this, write your own argument with the title 'Globalisation has more drawbacks than benefits'. Make sure you include reasons and evidence.

Figure 3.2: Poor working conditions are a drawback of globalisation

3   Now read this counter argument to the argument and answer the questions that follow.

Some argue that sweatshops in the developing world have generally been a good thing. Working conditions in clothes factories may often seem pretty awful, but they are better than a life of work in agriculture or having no job at all.

Many of the three million people working in sweatshops in Bangladesh are women, who, reportedly, have become more empowered than ever before. Although the minimum wage paid to workers in the clothes industry in Bangladesh may still seem low by standards in the western world, in 2010 it was still nearly double that of 2006. In September 2018, the Bangladesh government moved to raise the monthly minimum wage for garment workers – for the first time in five years – to USD 96, up from the previous USD 63, according to the Business and Human Rights Resource Centre (2018). The Bangladeshi economy has been growing every year, so we can conclude that life is getting better for people in Bangladesh.

CONTINUED

a   Do you think this counter argument is as strong as the argument above? Give reasons for your opinion.

b   What reasoning is used for the argument?

c   Does the author give any evidence to support the reasoning?

d   What else should you find out about before agreeing with the counter argument that globalisation is a benefit? For example, you might wish to consider the proportion of women employed in many factories in the developing world.

e   Share your answers about the strength of the counter argument with a partner. Do they give the same reasons as you?

> **TIP**
>
> You can use evidence to support a line of reasoning for an argument and to justify a claim.

3.2 Analysing claims and evidence

When you read or listen to arguments, it is useful to be able to recognise what **claims** are made by the writer or speaker, what evidence they give us to support their argument and what their **conclusions** are.

Analysing claims

In Activity 3.01 you read two short texts. One argued that there was no need to turn off the water while we brush our teeth. The second argued that we should turn off the water while we brush our teeth.

The first argument made a claim: 'It shouldn't matter if I do or not, since I'm only one person'. But the author gave no evidence to **justify** the claim – in other words, give reasons why it should be true.

The second argument made a claim that we can save water if we turn the water off. Look at the second argument again. Find the evidence that the author gave to convince us that this is true.

Figure 3.3 notes three claims related to global topics and Activity 3.03 looks specifically at claims about transport.

> **KEY TERMS**
>
> **claim:** a statement that something is true.
>
> **conclusion:** a reasoned judgement, a result, a final summary. You can come to a conclusion about something when you have looked at the evidence. You can also write a conclusion at the end of an essay, when you sum up your argument and answer the question.
>
> **justify:** to prove or give a good reason for something.

Crime is caused by unemployment.

Nuclear power is safe.

Child poverty is on the increase.

Figure 3.3: Claims related to global topics

ACTIVITY 3.03

1   Read the following list of claims about transport:

- Globally, more than twice as many men as women are injured in motor vehicle accidents.

- More serious motor vehicle accidents occur when it is raining than when it is snowing.

- Motor vehicle accidents injure more adults aged 18 to 24 than old people.

2   If you are working together as a class, or in a smaller group, take a vote on who thinks each of these claims is true or false. Record your results.

3   Individually or in pairs, take one of the claims each. Make a list of reasons why the claim might be true. For each of the reasons, search on the internet to see if you can find some evidence to support it.

4   Present the reasons and evidence you have been able to find to the rest of the group.

5   Finally, take the vote again on each of the claims. Are the results the same or different? Discuss together whether the reasons and evidence you have collected have changed your mind.

When discussing the claims, it is likely you at first thought that one claim was more believable than another, because you might have read something in a newspaper, seen it on the television or you might have heard others (for example, friends or family) talking about it.

'I heard it somewhere' is the reason generally given for people believing claims. If you agree about which claim was most believable, this is probably because you have both heard more about this than the other two.

People believe claims for the following reasons:

- It sounds believable.

- They trust the source.

- They hear the claim made from various sources.

- The claim is supported by experimental data (evidence).

Analysing evidence

When you are reading or listening to an argument, pay close attention to the evidence that the writer or speaker provides to support their claim. For example, this evidence might be in the form of a chart or table of statistics, as is the case in Activity 3.04. You should study the figures carefully, so that you can draw your own conclusions from the data and decide whether you agree or disagree with the claim that is being made.

ACTIVITY 3.04

1 Look at Tables 3.1 and 3.2. The data in these tables are collated by the Food and Agriculture Organization (FAO), an agency of the United Nations. Answer the questions that follow about the global topic Water, food and agriculture.

Table 3.1: Food exports, 2019 (USD million)

	Food (most categories)							All food
	Fruit and vegetables	Cereals and cereal preparations	Meat and meat preparations	Beverages	Dairy products and eggs	Fats and oils (excluding butter)	Sugar and honey	
World	274 386	193 411	155 647	114 205	84 981	81 748	41 987	1 382 462
Africa	16 032	2 491	800	1 647	847	2 240	2 816	52 798
Americas	79 208	57 170	53 002	18 236	7 562	13 829	12 944	369 800
Asia	78 076	37 584	14 858	14 121	6 616	34 826	11 365	309 809
Europe	95 352	89 511	70 028	76 195	57 823	29 751	13 187	593 343
Oceania	5 718	6 655	16 959	4 006	12 134	1 102	1 674	56 614

Table 3.2: Food imports, 2019 (USD million)

	Food (most categories)							All food
	Fruit and vegetables	Cereals and cereal preparations	Meat and meat preparations	Beverages	Dairy products and eggs	Fats and oils (excluding butter)	Sugar and honey	
World	278 390	20 908	151 189	115 037	86 769	87 127	44 669	1 412 037
Africa	6 649	28 275	5 368	3 114	4 824	9 690	6 726	80 927
Americas	60 475	38 271	22 723	36 335	7 881	12 047	8 316	264 684
Asia	79 018	78 004	61 910	24 289	26 766	36 851	15 326	485 353
Europe	129 247	59 442	59 722	48 734	45 860	27 697	13 558	560 832
Oceania	3 000	2 916	1 466	2 565	1 437	843	743	20 241

CONTINUED

a What evidence is there to support the claim that: 'In 2019, Africa's food imports cost more than it gained from food exports.'?

b What is the evidence to support the claim that: 'In 2019, Europe was the biggest importer of fruit and vegetables in the whole world.'?

c What evidence is there to support the claim that: 'The value of Oceania's food exports is higher than the cost of its food imports.'?

2 Discuss your answers to the questions with a partner. Does your partner agree with you?

3 Now, with your partner, take a few minutes to make three claims of your own that are related to the figures in the two FAO tables above.

Write down your claims and be ready to share them with the class. (You could make two correct claims and one incorrect claim to see if the rest of the class is paying attention.)

Figure 3.4: Coffee cherries being processed before export

3.3 Identifying and explaining facts, opinions, value judgements and predictions

When you read texts for interest or research, or to answer written questions, you will need to be able to tell the difference between facts, opinions, value judgements and predictions.

A lot of what we read and listen to is a mixture of fact and opinion. Being able to tell the difference between fact and opinion is important for evaluating written and spoken texts and developing persuasive arguments.

As a general rule, a fact can be proven, while an opinion is what someone thinks, feels or believes.

For example, a fact within the global topic of Education for all is: 'Educating girls helps to alleviate (lessen) poverty'. This is a fact because evidence from UNICEF shows that investing in girls' education transforms communities, countries and the entire world.

KEY TERMS

value judgement: a personal judgement about whether something is good or bad, right or wrong, based on personal beliefs or values.

prediction: a statement about what might happen in future.

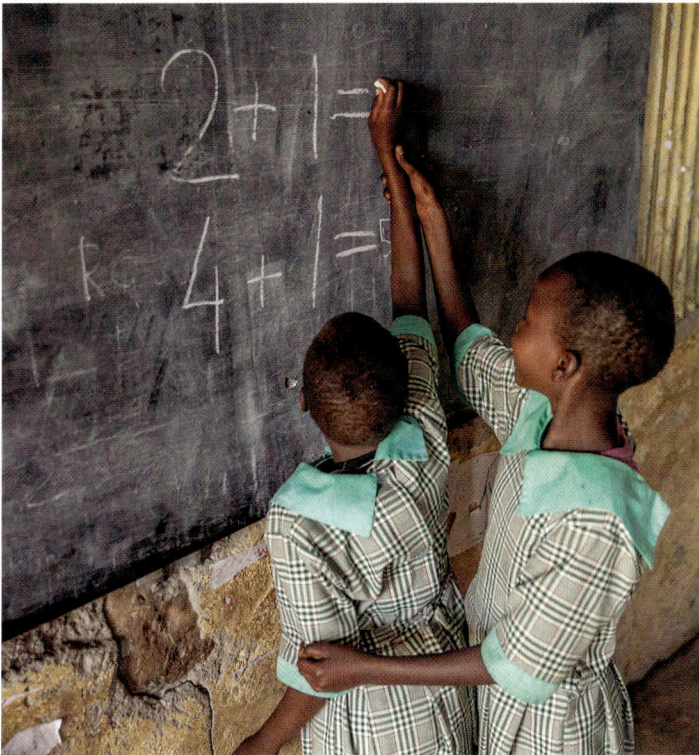

Figure 3.5: Educating girls transforms communities

Girls who receive an education are less likely to marry young and are more likely to lead healthy, productive lives. They earn higher incomes, participate in the decisions that affect them, and build better futures for themselves and their families.

The statement: '*All girls should stay at home and help their families*' is someone's opinion and cannot be proved to be true as there is no evidence to suggest it is true; it is simply someone's belief or what someone thinks or feels. However, in some cultures this is a strongly held belief that is enforced within communities.

DISCUSSION

With a partner, share your thoughts about which of these statements are facts and which are opinions.

a   The planet's climate has been warming over the past century.

b   We can do something about climate change.

c   Adults aged 18 to 24 are almost three times as likely as adults above this age to be unemployed.

d   The global recession has affected adults aged 18 to 24 the most all over the world.

e   It's easy to ride a bicycle.

f   Some international charities are excellent.

Can you state how you decided which was a fact and which was an opinion? It can be easier to identify facts first. These will contain something measurable which you can verify (check to see whether it is true or false). For example, '*Adults aged 18 to 24 are almost three times as likely as adults above this age to be unemployed*'. On the other hand, '*It's easy to ride a bicycle*' is true for some people but not others. Were there any which you found harder to decide using this method?

ACTIVITY 3.05

1   Look at the two statements below. One is a fact and one is an opinion. Which is which and how do you know?

   a   *'We served chicken to 50 customers yesterday.'*

   b   *'I believe that people should not eat chicken.'*

Discuss your ideas with a partner.

2   With your partner, read the following opinions and tell each other if you agree or disagree with them. Explain your reasons. Where do you think your ideas have come from? Do you think your ideas would be the same as everyone else's?

- Everyone should learn to read and write.

- Tea is bad for your health.

- Football is a very interesting and exciting game.

- After school, children should spend their time playing and relaxing, not doing schoolwork or studying.

- Going to art galleries and looking at paintings is a fun way to spend a day.

- Tennis is a really boring game.

- Teenagers should have part-time jobs to teach them the value of money.

- Mathematics is easy.

3   Choose one of the opinions you have discussed in part 2 of this activity. Write down the opinion which opposes it. For example, for 'Mathematics is easy' this would be 'Mathematics is difficult.' You and your partner should then take part in a debate. One of you should play the role agreeing with one opinion, and the other should play the role of agreeing with the opposing opinion. State your opinion, then give a reason to support it. Your partner should then state their opinion, give a reason to support it and also challenge your reason. For example:

- Mathematics is easy because most of the people in my class get good marks for their maths tests.

- Mathematics is difficult because most people lack the skills to deal with numbers. Even if most people in your class do well in maths tests, the majority of the population do not do so.

- Mathematics can be easy if it is taught using the right techniques, etc.

Keep going for at least five minutes, writing down your reasons and challenges as you go. Has this changed your mind on the issue, or changed your reasons for your opinion? This activity can be even more useful if you and your partner choose opinions that you would not normally agree with, but still try to defend them.

TIP

When debating an issue or presenting a spoken argument, there are many facts that most people take as given, such as the fact that the planet's climate has been warming over the past century, so you won't need to persuade people by finding a reliable source of information to prove this fact.

When writing an argument, however (for example, in a research report or essay), it is good practice to support each fact you quote with a reliable source of evidence.

While an opinion is what someone thinks, feels or believes, a value judgement is a little more. Value judgements consider the reasons why someone might think of something as right or wrong, or as good or bad.

The statement in the speech bubble is an example of a value judgement, because as well as an opinion ('*I don't think there should be major sporting events*'), the statement considers fairness. Here, fairness is seen as a good thing and moving people from their homes is seen as unfair, therefore bad.

> I don't think there should be major sporting events. It is just not fair to move people from their homes simply to accommodate a global sporting event like the Olympic Games.

An argument might also use prediction to support the points being made. A prediction can be made when there is evidence, or examples of the same event or issue occurring in the past. Predictions make claims about the future based on this knowledge. For example, '*South Africa experienced major droughts in 2004–2005, 2008–2009, 2015–2016 and in 2018–2020. It is therefore predicted that the region will again enter drought by 2023.*'

ACTIVITY 3.06

1   Read the text below, which relates to the topics of Health and wellbeing and Education for all, and identify the following:

- one fact
- one value judgement
- one opinion
- one prediction.

Once you have identified each, note down why you think your chosen text extract is a fact, opinion, value judgement or prediction.

Health Education

Most people would agree that health and education are the two most important services a country can provide. In recent years, many countries have been successful in reducing some of the most serious risks to children's health. Nowadays, children live longer and are healthier than in the twentieth century.

However, ill health still stops many children from going to school, and often it's because of a lack of health education within families. If we don't educate people in local communities about personal hygiene, they are more likely to become ill.

We need to ensure that health education is available for all families and not just for those that can afford it. Health education is a basic human right, and to not provide it for the most vulnerable in society is not acceptable.

CONTINUED

2   Discuss your responses with a partner. Did you agree?

Remember that sometimes there is more than one correct answer in a text of this length. As well as being able to identify a statement of argument, it is important that you can explain why you think a statement is a fact, opinion, value judgement or prediction.

Figure 3.6: Poor health stops many children going to school

TIP

When considering personal opinions and value judgements, you should be aware that they may not be objective. You will learn more about this in Chapter 4, Section 4.3 Bias and vested interest.

ACTIVITY 3.07

1   Read the following questions that might fall within the global topic of Environment, pollution and conservation. Which of these questions do you think will result in an answer that is: a fact, an opinion, a prediction or a value judgement?

    a   Are some animals more important than others?

    b   Where is the Great Barrier Reef?

    c   What will happen if humans continue to hunt and poach endangered species?

    d   Do you think that humans can enjoy a meat-free diet?

    e   Which is the largest ocean?

    f   Is it okay to wear a fur coat?

    g   What will happen to marine life if plastic continues to be dumped in the ocean?

2   Write down your answers to these questions. You may need to do some research for some of them.

3   Look at your answers and revisit part 1 of this activity to make any changes to the answers you originally gave for part 2.

4   Share your responses to the questions a to g with a partner. Try to explain why you think a certain question will get a certain type of information.

REFLECTION

What have you learned about analysing arguments and using counter arguments so far? How will you apply this knowledge in the future?

3.4 Comparing different arguments and perspectives

As you have seen in this chapter and you have probably noticed in real life, different people have different views and beliefs. They have different ideas about how we should live and how global problems should be solved.

When you are analysing or writing about global issues, and when you want to decide what you think about these issues, it is helpful to be able to compare different arguments and perspectives. This enables you to see which arguments and perspectives are stronger and more convincing and which ones you share.

TIP

Remember that arguments are stronger when they are more supported by reasoning and evidence. So when you are comparing arguments and perspectives to decide which is more convincing, you should consider:

- Are there reasons given?
- How closely do they support the conclusion?
- Is there evidence, and how relevant is it?

ACTIVITY 3.08

1   Read the text that follows. It relates to the topic of Poverty and inequality. The article explains how discrimination, violence and lack of access to resources such as healthcare have deepened the **inequality** experienced by **indigenous** communities. The author is making the claim that *'Indigenous people are among the most disadvantaged in society.'*

Indigenous people are among the most disadvantaged in society

There are 476 million indigenous people around the world and spread across more than 90 countries. They belong to more than 5000 different indigenous peoples and speak more than 4000 languages. Indigenous people represent about 5% of the world's population. The vast majority of them – 70% – live in Asia.

Although they have different customs and cultures, they face the same harsh realities: eviction from their ancestral lands, being denied the opportunity to express their culture, physical attacks and treatment as second-class citizens. Indigenous people are often marginalised[1] and face discrimination in countries' legal systems, leaving them even more vulnerable to violence and abuse. Indigenous human rights defenders who speak out face intimidation and violence, often supported by the state. In addition, individuals may be physically attacked and killed just for belonging to an indigenous people. Peaceful efforts by indigenous peoples to maintain their cultural identity or exercise control over their traditional lands, which are often rich in resources and biodiversity, have led to accusations of treason or terrorism.

Discrimination[2] is the reason why indigenous peoples make up 15% of the world's extreme poor.[3] Globally, they also suffer higher rates of landlessness, malnutrition and internal displacement than other groups. Indigenous women are less likely to use health care facilities when pregnant because of discrimination and mistreatment, and so they are more likely to die giving birth. For example, in Panama and Russia, indigenous women are about six times more likely to die in childbirth than women from the non-indigenous population. The birth rate for Amerindian adolescent girls is twice that of the general Guyanese population. In Kenya, Maasai women are twice as likely to have had no antenatal care, and in Namibia, San women are ten times more likely to give birth without skilled attendance.[4]

Around the world, indigenous peoples have been denied self-determination – a binding principle in international law which refers to peoples' right to freely determine their political status and freely pursue their economic, social and cultural development. Instead, indigenous peoples have suffered violence and oppression by both colonisers and mainstream society.

KEY TERMS

inequality: in a social context, the fact that some people or groups or countries have more opportunities, money, resources, power than other people, groups, or countries.

indigenous: indigenous people are groups who are connected by ancestry to a particular geographical area.

CONTINUED

During the nineteenth and twentieth centuries, Canada removed indigenous children from their families and placed them in federally funded boarding schools, with the intent of assimilating them into broader Canadian society. At these 'Indian Residential Schools'[5] they were not allowed to speak their languages or express their cultural heritage and identities. As a result, '*Aboriginal people were expected to have ceased to exist as a distinct people with their own governments, cultures, and identities*'[6]. An estimated 150 000[7] First Nations[8] children suffered abuse in these schools.

Aboriginal children in Australia were also forced to assimilate into white culture and were placed in institutions where they suffered abuse and neglect. These children are known as the 'Stolen Generations'.

References:

[1]United Nations Development Program (2022), 10 things we should all know about indigenous people (stories.undp.org)

[2]Amnesty International (2022), Discrimination (www.amnesty.org)

[3]United Nations (2022), People living in poverty (www.un.org)

[4]United Nations (2022), Indigenous women's maternal health and maternal mortality (www.un.org)

[5]National Centre for Truth and Reconciliation (2022), Reports (nctr.ca)

[6,7]National Centre for Truth and Reconciliation (2022), Residential School History (nctr.ca)

[8]The Canadian Encyclopedia (2022), First Nations (www.thecanadianencyclopedia.ca)

Source: www.amnesty.org

2 Copy the table below. (Leave space to add more rows later on if necessary.)

claim: '*Indigenous people are among the most disadvantaged in society*'			
	Reason for claim	Supporting evidence	Citation/Reference
1			
2			
3			

CONTINUED

3   Complete your table by listing three reasons given by the author to support the claim that 'Indigenous people are among the most disadvantaged in society' and adding any supporting evidence and references.

4   Share your information with a partner to see if you have the same information or if you can add to the information you have.

5   Looking at the information you have acquired, discuss with your partner whether you think the argument in the text is convincing.

Arguments that have supporting evidence from various sources are more convincing. Independently looking for evidence that supports a line of argument, such as causes and consequences, will help you look at multiple perspectives on the issue and make your argument stronger.

Figure 3.7: Indigenous people often face discrimination

ACTIVITY 3.09

Re-read the text in Activity 3.08 and work through the activity below with a partner.

1   How many causes and consequences can you find in the text in Activity 3.08?

2   Could you think of any other causes/other reasons why indigenous people might be disadvantaged?

CONTINUED

3   Do a little research on your own, putting the search term 'why are indigenous people disadvantaged?' into your browser and see what comes up. Try to identify two or three different causes or reasons. You might need to follow a link, or you may be able to identify some causes just from the titles of the articles (note down where you find them). Make notes of your findings.

4   Now, on your own, look for two or three consequences by putting in the search term: consequence/impact of indigenous disadvantage. (You could also look for 'consequence of' one of the causes you found.) Make notes of your findings.

5   Form groups of 4 or 5 to play the game "What if" by sharing your research findings and brainstorming possible solutions using the sentence beginning *What if…*

6   Act out two "what if" solutions (1 minute per scene). The first scene should demonstrate to the class "what if nothing is done" and the second scene should show a realistic, practical solution.

Combining evidence and working with others can also be useful to support your analysis. Reviewing the research and evidence as a group, or with another person, supports more effective decision-making and analytical skills than if you were to do it individually. Your peers can add their opinions and knowledge to the work and offer different perspectives and evidence from the multiple sources they have consulted for their research.

ACTIVITY 3.10

1   Working with a partner, choose one of the other examples of indigenous people from the text in Activity 3.08.

2   Use appropriate terms to search for information to further support the claim that: '*Indigenous people are among the most disadvantaged in society.*'

3   Add the information to the table you completed in Activity 3.08 by adding a further row (add more rows if you find more reasons and evidence).

4   Find someone in your class who chose a different group of indigenous people from the one you chose. Discuss the information you found to support the claim '*Indigenous people are among the most disadvantaged in society.*' Continue adding to the table you produced for Activity 3.08, as you find and discuss additional information.

3.5 Reaching a conclusion

After you have analysed the arguments or claims presented, and gathered your own evidence on the issue, the most important next step is to reach a conclusion. A conclusion is your considered view or opinion which you have come to after looking at all the facts and evidence.

Global warming is caused by human activity

More people in the world speak Chinese than any other language

Climate change is the result of global warming

Fossil fuels will run out one day

Overpopulation will impact on available resources

Figure 3.8: Drawing conclusions

Looking at the conclusions in Figure 3.8, they may appear to be the same as claims. However, conclusions are different from claims. You can make a claim without giving any evidence, but when you draw a conclusion, this will follow research and be based on the evidence you have found.

When you looked at the tables in Activity 3.04, you examined the evidence and drew conclusions. The two correct claims you made were conclusions you had drawn from the evidence. The incorrect claims you were also asked to make as part of the activity were not conclusions, because they were not based on evidence. Because the class could see the details in the tables, they could work out which claims were correct and which were not. If you were the only one with the information, they might believe you and jump to a conclusion that your claim was correct because they trust you.

> **TIP**
>
> It is easy to jump to conclusions without enough evidence – especially when the conclusion fits with our own beliefs and ideas, or is something we have heard before.
>
> Cambridge Global Perspectives is not about jumping to conclusions; it is about drawing conclusions based on evidence from different sources that come from different perspectives and looking at the viewpoints within these perspectives.

ACTIVITY 3.11

Figure 3.9: Some consequences of globalisation

1 Look at the images in Figure 3.9 related to the global topic of Globalisation.

   a Draw one conclusion about the setting of each image.
   (Where is this happening?)

   b Draw one conclusion about the relationships of the people in the pictures.
   (Who are the people in the images and how are they related?)

   c Draw one conclusion about the feelings of each person in the images.
   (What are they feeling? What are they thinking?)

2 Write a summary of your conclusions.

3 Share your summary with a partner. Discuss your thoughts.
   Do they agree with your conclusions? Are their conclusions different? If so, why do you think this is?

In Activity 3.11 you might have discussed whether any of your conclusions lacked enough support to be likely. You might need to find more (text-based) evidence before you can draw a reliable conclusion from an image. You might have been able to understand more clearly what was happening in the images by drawing conclusions. You might simply have jumped to conclusions without enough evidence.

Look again at the pictures in Figure 3.9. Which of the following topics could also be reflected in those pictures?

- Transport, travel and tourism.
- Poverty and inequality.
- Change in culture and communities.
- Law and criminality.
- Technology, industry and innovation.

The caption under the figure provides a **context**, or background, for your conclusions. When the caption says something different, this may change the way you look at the pictures.

KEY TERM

context: background, setting or circumstances that surround an idea or a statement and help you to understand it better.

Using conclusions to identify possible courses of action

If you are analysing an issue with a view to taking action on it, you should aim to identify several possible courses of action, analyse these carefully and conclude by selecting the one you feel would be effective and relevant, explaining why.

Figure 3.10: Select the most effective course of action

DISCUSSION

Read the text below on the topic of Conflict and peace, and identify which of the following conclusions reflect how Sam is feeling.

> Sam had a strong sense of loyalty and patriotism. He had always wanted to serve his country, but this was crazy. He was being sent to fight a war he knew very little about in a country a long way from home. He was supposed to help protect strangers and fight against an enemy he didn't even know. He was worried about being away from home and that he would not see his friends and family for a long time.

Conclusions:

A   Sam is a proud citizen of his country.

B   Sam is frightened of going to war.

C Sam wishes he had never joined the military.

D Sam is not looking forward to going abroad to fight.

What are the possible courses of action for Sam?

Figure 3.11: Conflict can result in incompatible or opposing needs, wishes or demands

SHOWCASING YOUR SKILLS

Analysis

Now you have the chance to use your skills to analyse texts and write answers to questions on them.

Read the two texts below and answer the questions that follow.

Source 1

Jamila

I believe that globalisation has made it easier to find out about other cultures by searching on the internet and by travelling more easily to other countries and cultures. I have made a lot of friends online. My online friends are from all over the world, and I chat to them every day. I have learned a lot about their lives and the food they eat and the music they like to listen to. Before the COVID-19 pandemic, I was planning to meet some of my friends when my family went on holiday to Europe. It is wonderful to share our cultures with people around the world online and in person as we can in the present time. By sharing ideas and interacting with each other, we understand other cultures and learn to respect them. My parents have raised me to believe that respecting others brings harmony and peace.

CONTINUED

Source 2

Some people believe that globalisation has made it easier to find out about other cultures by searching on the internet and by travelling more easily to other countries and cultures. Despite these benefits, the main argument against cultural globalisation is that it is causing the loss of cultural identity and languages. Some 600 languages have disappeared in the last century. According to UNESCO, there are 7000 languages spoken across the world but over 90% of them are under threat or at risk of disappearing. It is predicted that 3000 known languages may no longer be spoken by the end of this century. Nowadays, many people think that pop and westernised culture have destroyed the individuality of many other cultures. So maybe it's time to protect our languages and cultures if we don't want them to disappear.

Reference: UNESCO International Institute for Higher Education in Latin America and the Caribbean

In Source 1:

1   Identify a fact and an opinion given by Jamila.

2   Identify a value judgement. How do you know it is a value judgement?

3   How could the information in Source 1 impact on society as a whole?

In Source 2:

4   Identify an opinion given by the author.

5   Identify a piece of evidence presented by the author to support their claim that globalisation is causing a loss of languages.

6   How could the information in Source 2 impact on society as a whole?

In Sources 1 and 2:

7   Identify the main claims made by the two authors.

8   What are the perspectives of the two authors? Why do they disagree?

CONTINUED

Reflection on your showcase

Write a few lines describing what went well in your analysis of text:

Did you manage to answer all the questions?

Did you find it easy to identify facts and opinions?

Did you identify the main claims? Did this help you to understand the two perspectives?

What have you learned about comparing texts by analysing them?

Are you happy with your answers? What would you do differently another time?

SUMMARY

In Chapter 3 you have been thinking about and practising skills of analysis.

You have looked at arguments and thought about reasoning. You have identified a range of argument elements and practised analysing them.

You have thought about the difference between facts and opinions, identified predictions and value judgements, and discussed questions that might result in different types of answer. You have also considered how to use the results of your analysis to reach a conclusion.

You have used these skills to work on a comparison of two texts and answer written questions about them.

REVIEW AND REFLECTION

	I have learned about …	I need more practice with …
Analysing different issues and arguments		
Analysing claims and evidence		
Identifying and explaining facts, opinions, predictions and value judgements		
Comparing different arguments and perspectives		
Using the results of my analysis to reach a conclusion		

> Chapter 4
Evaluation

LEARNING INTENTIONS

In this chapter you will:

- Understand the importance of evaluation skills

- Evaluate reasoning and evidence in different arguments/perspectives

- Recognise bias and vested interest

- Understand some elements of credibility (reputation, expertise, experience, access to information)

- Evaluate written sources

- Understand how others' arguments/perspectives/credibility can affect your own perspective.

In this chapter you will learn how to evaluate both reasoning and evidence in different arguments and for different perspectives, identifying and assessing their strengths and their weaknesses. You will examine bias and vested interest, which will give you a useful tool for evaluating perspectives, as it provides one way of questioning sources to see whether they are more or less convincing. The chapter will also give you tools for evaluating the evidence for a source in even more detail, called credibility criteria. These include things like how well qualified the source is, whether they have experience of the issue and whether this matters. As well as evaluating a range of sources, you will be encouraged to question your own perspective and how it can be affected by the arguments of others.

Topics that will be explored in this chapter include Water, food and agriculture, Health and wellbeing (fast food), Education for all, Climate change, energy and resources, Migration and urbanisation, Globalisation, and Transport, travel and tourism.

KEY TERMS

bias: showing an inclination or prejudice for or against one person or group, especially in a way considered to be unfair.

vested interest: a personal reason for being involved in a project or situation, especially if it is for financial gain or recognition from others.

BEFORE YOU START

Copy and complete the following checklist based on what you have learned from Chapter 3, rating yourself out of 5 on each of the skills:

Skill	Rating out of 5
I can identify an argument and the elements of which an argument is made up.	
I know the difference between a fact and an opinion.	
I can recognise a value judgement.	
I can compare texts and draw conclusions from this.	

4.1 Why we need evaluation skills

Evaluation is a very useful skill in everyday life and in study and research. When you evaluate something, you look at its strengths and weaknesses. You think about whether it is working and does what is intended. When you read product reviews, they include evaluations of the product. If you evaluate an argument, you think about whether you are convinced by the argument, whether it makes sense and is logical and whether the author supports their claims with convincing and appropriate evidence.

DISCUSSION

When might you use evaluation in your everyday life? Think about the way you discuss TV programmes, or electronic devices, or games. Do you ever read reviews? Hold a class discussion about product reviews and how they show evaluation.

Figure 4.1: Product reviews are based on an evaluation of their strengths and weaknesses

You will have to evaluate source material when you are carrying out research, whether you are working individually or in a team. You could be asked to evaluate source material and the evidence used to support claims, arguments and perspectives within source material. There will also be situations where you will need to complete written reflections about your experiences. Reflection and evaluation generally go together, so when you write reflections, you will need to use your evaluative skills.

ACTIVITY 4.01

Read the following example of a reflection on teamwork. The writer is evaluating their teamwork.

> The team worked well together. I think this was because we all knew each other beforehand, and we knew each other's strengths so we could easily decide who was going to do what.

The first sentence is an observation about how well the team worked together. This is the evaluation. The second sentence is a reflection on why someone thought the team worked well. This explains and supports the evaluation.

1   Imagine that the first sentence said, 'The team did not work well together.' Now rewrite the second sentence to explain why the team did not work well.

2   Share your version of the second sentence with a partner. Did you come up with similar thoughts?

Evaluation is a higher-level skill, so the ability to evaluate well will be useful not only for Cambridge Global Perspectives, but also for other subjects, for higher education and for life in general.

4.2 Evaluating perspectives and arguments

You have already discussed product evaluation and started to think about evaluating teamwork. Now you are going to start practising evaluating perspectives and arguments. First you will look at evaluating evidence and reasoning.

When you evaluate a perspective or argument to decide if it is convincing, you will need to look at the evidence the writer provides to support what they are saying. You will also need to look at the reasoning: is there a logical argument that you can follow?

When you evaluate perspectives or arguments, you should assess both the strengths and the weaknesses of evidence and reasoning. Remember, however, that you need to do this in context. Think of evaluation as a bit like a product review. When you look at product reviews, you need to keep in mind what you will be using the product for. An example would be a computer. Do you want it for surfing the internet and doing schoolwork and social networking with friends? Or are you a keen gamer? If you are looking for a good gaming computer, you will have different requirements, so you will need different specifications. You will evaluate different computers to see which has the strengths you need.

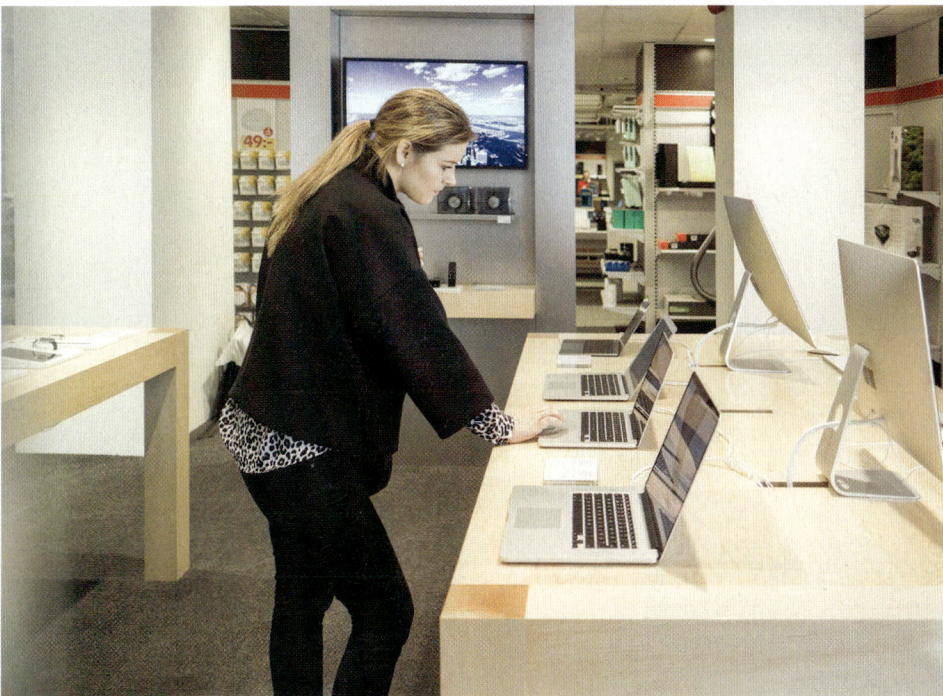

Figure 4.2: Which is the best for me?

The same is true when evaluating evidence and reasoning. You might see a lot of facts and figures in a text, but when you look at them carefully you could find that they are not relevant to the issue, or they do not really support the author's claims. Or that the author suggests a solution to an issue, but when you think about it, you realise that their suggestion would not really make a difference to the issue you are researching.

When you have evaluated a perspective or argument, you should always be able to give explanations for your evaluation. Try starting with 'The evidence for this claim is weak because …' or 'The reasoning is strong because …'. To make sure you can give explanations, you should decide how you will assess the evidence and always include a reason for your decision.

Evaluating evidence and reasoning for a perspective

When evaluating evidence and reasoning for a perspective (global, national or local) or a viewpoint within a perspective (for example, that of a scientist, politician or teacher), consider:

- Is evidence for the perspective provided? If so, does it actually support the perspective?

- Is the reasoning only based on opinion, anecdotal evidence or value judgements?

- Is hard data provided in support of the perspective?

For example, when the United Kingdom voted in 2016 on whether to leave the European Union, members of the population held widely different views (Figure 4.3).

Figure 4.3: This 'Remain' supporter (left) and 'Brexit' supporter (right) have different perspectives

ACTIVITY 4.02

Read the argument that follows (it relates to the topic Education for all) and answer the questions below.

Argument for free primary education for all

Education is vital for ending world poverty. With education, there are more employment opportunities, income levels are increased and there is an improvement in the health of children generally. In regions where access, attendance and the quality of education have seen improvements, there has also been a decline in the spread of HIV/AIDS and an increase in the health of the community in general. In fact, children of women who are educated are more likely to live past the age of five. Not only does education improve individual and family health, it also improves community health. In countries with good education systems, there is greater economic growth and a lower crime rate.

Figure 4.4: Education is vital for ending world poverty

1   Is a clear viewpoint expressed?

2   Is there evidence to support the claims made, and how strong is this evidence?

3   Are the claims to support the viewpoint presented in a logical way? (Do they make sense?)

4   Are there any weaknesses in the evidence and/or reasoning?

Evaluating evidence and reasoning in an argument

When evaluating evidence and reasoning in an argument, consider whether:

- there is a clear statement of an idea or a viewpoint with enough supporting evidence

- ideas are presented in a logical and connected way

- there are any weaknesses and **fallacies** in the evidence and reasoning, for example a mismatch between cause and effect.

KEY TERM

fallacy: an error in reasoning or a mistaken idea.

ACTIVITY 4.03

1   Read the following evaluation of an argument with the title 'Fast food causes obesity', which could fall under the topic Water, food and agriculture or Health and wellbeing. (Note: you are only reading the evaluation, not the original argument.)

> The author claims that fast food causes obesity. The argument is weak because they do not support it with evidence about the link between fast food and obesity. All the evidence the author provides is about the ingredients in fast food and how they are unhealthy. The author does not explain how fast food causes obesity, so the reasoning is also weak. There is some strong evidence about the link between fast food and heart disease, but this is not what the author is claiming. So the author's evidence is not really relevant and the argument is not convincing.

Why does the writer of this evaluation think that the author's evidence is not relevant? Why does the writer think that makes the argument weaker? Write down your answers and compare with a partner.

2   Read the following text on a similar theme.

Fast food is bad for kids' learning

A new study published in the *Clinical Pediatrics Journal* (2014) suggests that children who eat regularly at McDonald's, KFC, Pizza Hut and the like don't perform as well at school as their peers.

'*Research has been focused on how children's food consumption contributes to the child obesity epidemic,*' Kelly Purtell, who led the study at Ohio State University, told the *Telegraph*. '*Our findings provide evidence that eating fast food is linked to another problem: poorer academic outcomes.*'

The study used data from a sample of 8544 American schoolchildren, measuring their fast-food consumption at the age of 10 and then – after attempting to account for other factors – comparing that against academic results in reading, maths and science at the age of 13.

In science, for example, those kids that never ate fast food scored 83 points, compared to an average of 79 points for those who ate it every day. According to the *Telegraph*, theories about this are based on brain chemistry – such as a lack of iron, which leads to slower development, the effects of sugars in the diet and so on.

Source: qz.com

CONTINUED

Evaluate the evidence and reasoning presented for the argument *'Fast food is bad for kids' learning.'*

You can do this by copying out and completing the following table. The first row has been filled in for you. Add as many rows as you need.

Reasoning/evidence	Strength	Weakness
Children who eat regularly at McDonald's, KFC or Pizza Hut do not perform as well at school	Makes specific comparison which is relevant to conclusion on children's learning	Does not provide a measurement of the impact on learning

ACTIVITY 4.04

1   With a partner, read the following source on the topic of Climate change, energy and resources and discuss the questions that follow.

Source 1

> We know that fossil fuels are going to run out soon and that we need to find alternatives. We need to be thinking about these alternatives now. Nuclear power is the best alternative because nuclear power produces more energy than fossil fuels. Research shows that a pound of nuclear fuel produces about one million times the energy of a pound of fossil fuel.

a   What do you think the main argument of the whole text is? (This is only part of the whole text.)

b   What is the author reasoning here?

c   Is there any evidence to support the reasoning?

CONTINUED

Figure 4.5: Moving away from fossil fuels to produce energy

2   Now, with your partner, read Source 2, which contains a counter argument to the use of nuclear power and then discuss the questions.

Source 2

> Nuclear power cannot be an alternative to fossil fuels for energy as it's not safe. Just look at the nuclear disasters that have happened around the world! Surely, it would be safer to replace fossil fuels with wind and solar power, wouldn't it?

a   What is the author reasoning in Source 2?

b   Is there any evidence to support the reasoning?

c   Do you think the reasoning in Source 2 is better or worse than the reasoning in Source 1? Explain your answer.

In Activity 4.04, the author is arguing for alternatives to using fossil fuels for energy (because fossil fuels will run out). Source 1 is reasoning that more energy is obtained from nuclear power than from burning fossil fuels. Evidence from research does support the reasoning, but this is not very strong evidence because the text does not tell us exactly which research and when the research was done, or who did it.

You may have decided that the reasoning was weaker in Source 2 as there is not as much evidence to support it. The reason given for not using nuclear energy is that it is not safe. The author mentions that nuclear disasters have happened 'around the world' but does not give us any examples at all. There is also no reasoning given for the statement about using wind and solar power. The support in Source 2 is too vague and general.

ACTIVITY 4.05

Read the article that follows, which relates to the topic of Migration and urbanisation, and highlight the evidence provided.

Complete this table as you read, filling in your evaluative comments. For example, is there enough evidence to support the point being made? Is it convincing evidence? You may wish to copy out the table before you start to read.

Identify:	Evaluative comments
Claim	
Evidence	
Perspective	
Course of action recommended	
Is this a good argument? Is there a conclusion? Is the conclusion supported by the evidence?	
Write a short sentence to evaluate the source used in this passage.	

CONTINUED

Europe must take responsibility in migration crisis: Parliament head

By *DAILY SABAH* ANKARA 28 November 2021 – 1:13 p.m. GMT+3

'Europe has to take responsibility for the migration crisis and fulfill its humanitarian *duty,'* Turkish Parliament Speaker Mustafa Şentop said on Sunday.

...

'There are millions of migrants in the world who have to leave their countries. Migration from countries such as Syria and Afghanistan is being experienced a lot, especially in Europe, which includes Turkey.'

...

Noting that the immigration problem has increased as a result of the actions of the United States and parts of Europe in countries such as Afghanistan, Syria, Libya and Iraq, and that these countries bear the greatest responsibility, Şentop said, *'However, these countries are taking zero responsibility and it is unacceptable.'*

...

This year alone, the United Nations officials estimate that 1,600 people have died or gone missing in the Mediterranean Sea, the main gateway to Europe for migrants trying to enter the continent with the help of human smugglers.

...

'In the world we live in, we cannot say that some countries have only responsibilities, while others have only rights. I would like to remind Europe that in the face of these humanitarian crises, they owe a debt of conscience and humanity to the people of the world they used to exploit.'

...

Figure 4.6: Immigration by sea can be perilous

In recent years, hundreds of thousands have made short but perilous journeys across the Aegean Sea to reach northern and western Europe in search of a better life.

Hundreds of people have died at sea as many boats carrying refugees sank or capsized. The Turkish Coast Guard Command has rescued thousands of others.

...

International refugee protection agreements dictate that people should not be expelled or returned to a country where their life and safety might be in danger, due to their race, religion, nationality, or membership in a social or political group.

Source: www.dailysabah.com

KEY TERM

humanitarian: connected with improving human lives and reducing suffering.

4.3 Recognising bias and vested interest

Paris is the most interesting city in the world.

People like me who own holiday homes are providing jobs for local people.

My uncle's restaurant serves the best Thai food in the whole of Australia.

The government is always right, I know, I work for it!

Another way to evaluate arguments and perspectives is to think about the possible feelings and motives of the author. When you research information, or read news articles or listen to people speaking about topics of interest, you need to know who is telling you about the information. Can you trust them? Are they reliable?

If you think about everyday life, parents can sometimes have an unrealistic view of their own children. Why is this? Why do people often think their own family, or town, or country is better than others? This feeling is called bias. Bias is like prejudice. Our feelings get in the way of being logical and fair. We may say more about the positives of people we like and more about the negatives of people we do not like. We might not give a balanced view if we are biased.

Bias is not always conscious or deliberate; we often do not realise we are biased. We are just positive about people we like without noticing it. We make excuses for their weaknesses because we like them. Being biased makes us unreliable.

Vested interest is a bit similar. Vested interest can also lead to unreliability. However, vested interest is not really about feelings so much as about personal gain, or possibility of personal loss. A good example would be an employee of a car company speaking publicly about the cars their company makes. It is likely that the employee would say good things about the cars in public.

Think about that example. What could the employee gain by saying good things about their company's products? What could they lose if they said that the cars made by their company were no good?

DISCUSSION

Consider the restaurant sign in Figure 4.7 – the kind of sign you might see on a main road between two towns. Would you go to this restaurant if you were on holiday? Why?

Figure 4.7: Restaurant sign

Discuss the restaurant sign with a partner and the reason(s) why you might turn right. How does this sign show bias and/or vested interest?

ACTIVITY 4.06

With a partner, choose a role play for an everyday situation that has bias/vested interest in it. In your chosen role you get two minutes to make your partner see your perspective and convince them, using a well-structured argument.

You are selling used cars. The car you are trying to sell is the worst one in the yard, but if you sell it, your boss has promised you four weeks extra holiday.	You own a restaurant and a customer is not happy with their meal. They have said they will leave a negative review on the internet about your restaurant. You don't want to give them a free meal but you also don't want the negative review.
You are selling a city tour to tourists. You need to book one more person onto the tour and you will receive a bonus in your wages.	You are a gaming designer. You have realised that you have only included male characters in the game, although you know that 50% of the customers are female. Your boss wants an explanation from you.

ACTIVITY 4.07

Read the following two perspectives on vegan diets:

Perspective 1

According to the United Nations, a vegan diet is more sustainable and less demanding on the environment than a meat- and/or dairy-based diet, with a vegan diet taking about 10% of the resources – land, water, fuel, etc. – to maintain. So from an ecological perspective, veganism is the best option for the future – our world resources can sustain a much larger population as vegans than omnivores.

Source: www.theguardian.com

Perspective 2

Ah, climate change. Will Veganism save the planet by killing off methane-emitting farm animals? Ruminants do indeed produce methane, but then so does rice; methane from rice farming causes 3% of anthropogenic [caused by humans] global warming. Methane from grazing cows, however, is recycled into the soil by being broken down into CO_2 and absorbed by new grass. Unlike the methane produced by water-logged paddies. If the Vegan prophecies scare you, it's worth mentioning that seaweed additives for cattle may reduce emissions by 82% according to new findings from researchers at the University of California, Davis.

Source: www.unherd.com

Copy and complete the following table which will help you to compare and evaluate the two perspectives.

Perspective 1	Perspective 2
Evidence of bias or vested interest	Evidence of bias or vested interest
Strong reasoning	Strong reasoning
Weak reasoning	Weak reasoning
I find Perspective ___ more convincing because…	

TIP

When drawing conclusions, it is important that you use evidence for conclusions from different sources and perspectives to avoid bias and/or vested interest.

ACTIVITY 4.08

Read the text below and answer the questions that follow.

> The school has a really good reputation and some famous people have graduated from there – politicians and business people. It has an amazing history. It is also set in beautiful grounds and the sports facilities are excellent. It is a very good school and provides a high standard of education. This school really just caters for local families. As we live nearby, my son should get a place there next year.

This text may be completely accurate, but it seems to be biased.

1   Look carefully at the language and identify what seems biased.

2   From what the author tells us, why might they be biased about this school?

3   Share your answers with a partner. Do you think that you have both understood what bias is?

4.4 Evaluating credibility and reliability

When we evaluate the arguments we read, we consider the reasoning and logic of the argument. We also consider whether the author might be biased or have a vested interest. In addition, we can consider how believable the author's argument or information is, based on what we know about the author themselves.

When we assess an author's believability we can apply a series of tests which are sometimes called **credibility** criteria. Credibility simply refers to the believability of an author – how truthful we think what they say is.

The following are some of the credibility criteria which are most often applied to sources.

The **reputation** of a source is simply how they are seen by others. If a source has a good reputation then a large number of people have previously reported that they have been able to rely on the information they have provided. For example, the Associated Press is regarded as having a reputation for providing accurate and impartial news reporting. Just because a source has a good reputation does not necessarily mean that its information can always be trusted, but it is a factor we can consider.

We can also think about a source's **expertise**. Sources of information do not necessarily have to be written by an expert. However, in some situations, if the author has had specialised training or gained qualifications, it might put them in a position to be able to provide more trustworthy information. For example, if you were feeling

KEY TERM

credibility: the credibility of a source refers in general to how believable the author is and how much we can rely on what they say.

reputation: what people say or think about a person or an organisation. If someone has a good reputation, you might trust them and, also, they might be honest because they want to keep their good reputation.

expertise: the skill of an expert. Expertise can be gained by study, training or experience, or a combination of all of these. You might trust someone who is trained to do a job more than someone who has no training or has not studied the area.

ill would you feel more confident in asking your friend or a qualified medical doctor to diagnose you? Would you feel more confident if your biology teacher had studied science at university? When we consider these questions we are thinking about expertise.

Figure 4.8: Some sources are more credible than others

We might also ask about the **experience** of a source. This can often go along with expertise, but is simply how much familiarity they have built up in the area they are talking about. Charities working in areas of long-term food poverty, for example sub-Saharan Africa, are more credible because of their experience – they have worked for many years in that area and have been able to collect a lot of evidence about what things are really like.

Access to information/knowledge should also be considered. Is a source able to access the information that is relevant to the claims they are making? If the police are investigating a crime, they will always prefer to get evidence from an eye-witness who actually saw what happened rather than someone else who has an opinion which is not based on the direct evidence of what has happened. This can apply to secondary sources too – have they been able to access and read the sources of evidence they are using to support their claims?

All of these factors should be applied to the authors of sources we come across in our research when we are deciding how credible they are. Remember also to consider the evidence itself in their arguments. When we do this we refer to its **reliability**: whether we can find evidence in similar sources which back it up, or if it is used by other sources which have proved to be credible.

KEY TERMS

experience: practical knowledge or skills learned over time and with practice or from life events. Most skills can be improved with practice, and we can learn from the things that happen to us. You might trust someone who has experience with your problem.

access to information/ knowledge: this can be part of expertise. It is concerned with what a source knows or can find out. Do they have the information already, if not, can they get the information?

reliability: the trustworthiness of evidence. You might decide the information in a source is reliable because it has proved to be reliable in other circumstances, or because others have told you it is reliable.

ACTIVITY 4.09

Take a few minutes to think about who you would trust to give you accurate information and/or guidance about the following.

As you decide, think about why you would trust them. You may think of more than one person and more than one reason for each.

- Your own health
- How to do well in your tests at school or end of year exams
- The best smartphone
- How to make pancakes
- Cyber addiction
- Where the nearest cinema is (in a strange town or city)

- How to get fit and strong
- How to get a stain out of a shirt
- The correct dosage of any medication
- Fashionable clothes
- Bullying
- How to get help with stress.

Note down your ideas, ready to share them with the class.

Figure 4.9: Who would you go to for advice?

REFLECTION

Reflect on what you have been learning about evaluation so far. How will evaluating credibility and reliability help you in the future? Could you apply this knowledge to other subject areas you study?

4.5 Evaluating written sources

When you research written material, such as websites, books, articles or newspapers, for example for an individual research report or essay, you will have to analyse and evaluate these sources to make sure they are suitable and relevant for your needs. In general, information that is published by credible sources, such as newspapers and journal articles in magazines, is easy to evaluate. Websites can be more difficult to evaluate as information included on the website may not be accurate or credible. When you write your report, you should give **references** for the sources you have used in your research and quoted in your essay. You are also responsible for making sure your sources are accurate in what they claim. When you evaluate your sources, you need to explain how they supported your research and whether they are good sources to use.

You are now going to learn how to evaluate written sources in detail, starting with websites. You will do this by completing a checklist which will allow you to systematically go through the criteria for evaluation. These criteria can also be applied to other written sources.

> **KEY TERM**
>
> **reference:** when you give a reference in a piece of written work, you acknowledge the use of a source of information that you used.

ACTIVITY 4.10

1 Choose a well-known celebrity and search online for any brands or products they endorse. You may also need to follow links to product websites to find enough information. Copy and complete the table below to evaluate the source.

Criteria	Web sources	Yes/No	Evaluation notes
Accuracy	Is the information free from errors in spelling, grammar, etc?		
	Are charts and graphs clearly labelled and easy to read?		
	Are there links to other credible sources that can back up the information?		
Authority	Who is responsible for the web page?		
	Is the person/organisation responsible for the web page an expert in their field?		
Objectivity	Is there any advertising on the website? If so is it clear what it is advertising and what the content of the website is?		
	Are opinion pieces clearly labelled as such?		
Currency	Is there a date to show when the web page was written?		
	Are there signs that the work is kept up to date?		
Coverage	Is the page complete or under construction?		
	Is the entire source on the web or only part of it?		

CONTINUED

2   Find someone in your class who has chosen a similar source to you for this activity and discuss each of the criteria.

3   Overall, do you think the web source that you have chosen is a reliable and credible source of information? Give reasons for your answer. Make a note of these reasons.

4   Write a paragraph to evaluate the source you have chosen, using the information from your table and the reasons you gave.

Remember that when you are evaluating any source, you should consider the strengths and weaknesses of that source in relation to the question you want to answer or the specific argument you wish to make, for example whether nuclear power is a suitable replacement for fossil fuels. As well as identifying each strength and weakness, you should try to develop your answers by justifying why you think the point you mention is a strength or weakness.

ACTIVITY 4.11

1   Read the following text about the topic of Globalisation. Think about whether this source wants you to agree or disagree with what it says. What groups of people might disagree with what it says? How many other perspectives are represented? Decide whether you think the source is a good source to use to support arguments in favour of globalisation.

> Globalisation has many benefits. It can bring wealth to some of the world's poor. For example, a lot of South-East Asia was really poor not so long ago, but thanks to international trade, many of these countries now experience growth. The United Nations provides many statistics on their website that support this. This means people are much better off now than their parents and grandparents were.
>
> Globalisation also helps protect the environment. Some people have suggested that in the past countries could produce as much pollution as they wanted to, but nowadays, if they want to join the global marketplace, other countries can put pressure on them to clean up their act. I have seen how some countries are now thinking more about environmental protection in my work at the environmental protection agency.
>
> *Source: Adapted from an international trade magazine*

2   With your partner have a short debate – one person arguing that this is a good source to use, and one arguing this is not a good source to use. Use the questions in the first part of the activity to help you.

TIP

When evaluating sources, always give a reason why you think an aspect of a source is a particular strength or weakness. Starting with the phrase 'This is a weakness because' or 'This is a strength because' will help you to justify your evaluation.

When evaluating sources, remember to consider:

- Who wrote the information?

- Is the information likely to be biased, inaccurate or one-sided?

- Are experts quoted and, if so, who are the experts? Are they credible?

- Do other sources support the claims?

You may have noted in Activity 4.11 that the argument on globalisation is one-sided as it comes from a trade magazine, so just gives the benefits rather than any disadvantages of globalisation. Few sources of information are given, although the United Nations is cited, and this might make the article more credible. No other sources of evidence are cited. The author works for an environmental protection agency, so the evidence given might be credible, but there are few specific examples. For these reasons, you could decide that this source is useful for supporting the argument for globalisation but that you would need to find other sources to add to the information here or to provide further evidence for the argument.

ACTIVITY 4.12

1   Using the search terms 'poverty', 'Orissa', 'India' and 'video', find and watch a short video-clip about the landless people in Orissa, India.

2   Answer the following questions:

   a   Do you think the source is reliable and credible?
       Give reasons for your answer.

   b   What conclusions can be drawn from the video-clip?

   c   Are there any examples of bias and/or vested interest in the clip?

   d   What course of action is suggested to help resolve the situation?

3   Discuss your answers to questions a to d with a partner.

4.6 Considering the impact of the arguments/perspectives/credibility on your own perspective

In Section 4.5, you considered who you would trust to give you advice and information on a range of issues.

When you are researching different perspectives and looking at different sources to find information about an issue, you will need to take into consideration whether you are convinced by the arguments put forward by your sources and whether you find their perspective reasonable.

Then you will make up your own mind about the issue you have researched. You will base your own perspective on how convincing the evidence provided for each argument is and how convincing the different perspectives are. If you are convinced by the evidence and the arguments provided, you are more likely to agree with what they say – this is called a 'preferred' reading. However, this might not always be the case. Rejecting other perspectives and arguments and creating your own based on what you think is called an 'oppositional' reading. This can also happen when your own beliefs conflict with perspectives you have researched. You might also have a 'negotiated' reading when you make up your own mind, which means you accept some of the arguments and perspectives, but you reject some of the others as well.

Consider Figure 4.10 as an example of a negotiated reading. The child understands the arguments that he should eat his vegetables (the preferred reading) but has chosen to reject these perspectives, until he is offered the broccoli, which he really likes. His reading of the situation and the position he takes have switched from being oppositional to negotiated.

When you write about your research, you should explain how your thinking has changed or developed as a result of researching an issue. You may find that your own perspective changes when you explore other people's perspectives, learn more about the issue and read different arguments. Alternatively it is possible that researching an issue will strengthen your opinion and give you a more developed perspective.

Figure 4.10: A negotiated reading – where some ideas are accepted and some are rejected

ACTIVITY 4.13

Read the following two extracts from longer documents. They are both on the topic of Transport, travel and tourism, in particular about aviation. They agree about some things, but their solutions are different.

Read them through carefully and then decide which one you like more. Which one is more convincing? Which one is easier to read? There are some questions to answer after the two documents.

Source 1 is an excerpt from the website of the International Air Transport Association (IATA), which is the trade association for the world's airlines. This is what it says about aviation:

Source 1

Net zero 2050: new aircraft technology

The aviation industry's net-zero carbon emissions target is focused on delivering maximum reduction in emissions at source, through the use of sustainable aviation fuels (SAF), innovative new propulsion technologies, and other efficiency improvements (such as improvements to air traffic navigation).

The fuel-efficiency of aircraft has been consistently improving since the first passenger jets were introduced in the 1950s. Each new generation of plane has reduced emissions by around 15–20%. The overall fuel efficiency of the fleet is around 80% better than 50 years ago. The incremental improvements brought

Figure 4.11: Will more efficient planes help the carbon footprint?

over time have principally come from more efficient engines, better aerodynamics, and reduced weight. The use of composites instead of aluminium in the latest generation of planes has brought weight down, allowing engines to operate more efficiently.

Hybrid-electric concepts combine the advantages of both combustion and electric engines. The combustion and electric propulsion systems can be used in combination during take-off to provide maximum thrust, and the combustion engine can be throttled back when the aircraft is in cruise flight or descending. Combustion engines could also be smaller and reduce on-board weight. Hybridisation is a necessary intermediate step for larger airplanes towards a pure electric propulsion system. Hybrid-electric aircraft on a new airframe body such as the Blended Wing Body can contribute to achieving CO_2 reductions of up to 40%. Small aircraft (15–20 seats) with hybrid-electric propulsion are expected during this decade, regional aircraft in the 2030s and possibly larger ones from 2040. Norway has the goal of operating all domestic and shorthaul flights electrically by 2040.

Hydrogen is a carbon-free fuel that can be used as a propulsion fuel for combustion in conventional engines, replacing jet fuel (including in large aircraft), and also in fuel cells for electrical power. The weight of hydrogen is three times lower than that of an amount of jet fuel with the same energy content, but its volume even in liquid (cryogenic) form is four times larger. Much larger tanks as well as fundamental changes in the aircraft fuel system are therefore needed. One of the biggest challenges for hydrogen use in aviation is its availability at large scale, the need to produce 'green' hydrogen and the existence of appropriate supply infrastructure. Interest is growing however, and technology programmes now envisage entry into service around 2035.

CONTINUED

The development of new aerodynamic designs for commercial airplanes could create significant efficiency improvements and make it easier for alternative propulsion systems to succeed.

Here are three potential examples: Canard wing: Already used in military airplanes, canard-wing planes create low-drag through the main wing being set further back behind small forewings. Blended wing: Wide airfoil-shaped bodies and efficient high-lift wings enable significant lift-to-drag ratio improvements compared with conventional aircraft. High fuel savings are generated as the entire plane is designed to generate lift. Strut or truss-braced wing: Utilises a structural wing support to allow for larger wing spans without increases in weight. By increasing the span the induced drag is reduced and therefore the engine performance requirements can be reduced. The high wings allow for larger engine sizes.

Source: www.iata.org

Source 2 is an extract from an article on the *Scotsman* newspaper website written by Angela Terry, a green campaigner and consumer expert. In it she suggests 'how you can take simple, practical steps to help save the planet'. This is what she says about aviation:

Source 2

Stay grounded.

Aviation accounts for around 2.4% of global carbon emissions.

Including other gases and vapour trails produced by aircraft, the industry is responsible for roughly 5% of greenhouse gas emissions.

This might not seem like a big deal, until you consider that, despite the climate emergency, the airline industry plans to grow. Also, only a small percentage of people in the world actually fly at all.

In 2018, before the pandemic restricted travel, only 11% of the global population flew.

In Britain, 15% of the population take 70% of flights. These frequent flyers are causing considerable harm. It clearly isn't fair, especially when the climate crisis is already hitting the poorest people hardest, who don't even have the option of flying.

The truth is, taking a flight will raise your carbon footprint very quickly. Reducing the amount you fly, the distance you fly, or cutting air travel out altogether, is a way of making a meaningful contribution to tackling global warming.

Source: www.edinburghnews.scotsman.com

CONTINUED

1   Answer the following questions comparing the two sources:

    a   What are the two perspectives on aviation being presented?

    b   Give one or two similarities between the two sources.

    c   Which source is easier to understand? Why?

    d   What reading do you have of the sources: preferred, oppositional or negotiated? Explain your choices and your perspective on each source.

    e   Which source has more or stronger evidence?

    f   Is the reasoning better in one source? Or are the two sources different but with equally strong reasoning?

    g   Which author do you think is more credible? Think about expertise/experience/ knowledge – you may have to look up the authors on the internet to decide.

2   Discuss your answers with a partner or in a group.

SHOWCASING YOUR SKILLS

Evaluation

For this showcase, you can choose either Option A or Option B.

Option A

Work in a group. Each group will revisit one section from this chapter on evaluation.

As a group you will prepare a presentation. This can be a role-play, a demonstration, a mini lesson, a group talk or an activity.

Your group will explain and illustrate to the rest of the class the aspect of evaluation that you have been asked to focus on. You can select part of the section, or all of it.

All of you should be involved in both the preparation and the presentation to the class. You can divide the presentation up so that each one of you has something to do or say.

Option B

Select three sources that have information about globalisation. You should find a source from a website, a national newspaper/magazine, or a journal article from the internet. For each, write a paragraph to evaluate the source. You can look back at the work you have already done on evaluating sources, to remind yourself of the sorts of comments you might make.

CONTINUED

Reflection on your showcase

Option A

Write a few lines describing what went well in your group's evaluation presentation.

Was the presentation successful? How do you know?

What was difficult?

How could you improve things for next time?

Did you enjoy the other presentations?

Did this activity help you to revise what you have learned in this chapter?

Option B

Write a few lines describing what went well in your source evaluation.

Did you manage to evaluate your sources?

Did you find different things to say about different sources?

What have you learned about source evaluation?

Are you happy with your work? What would you do differently another time?

SUMMARY

In Chapter 4 you have been thinking about and practising evaluation of arguments and sources.

You have looked at some examples of bias and vested interest. You have considered what makes sources believable or trustworthy (credible/reliable).

You have thought about the ways your own perspective can be affected by others' arguments and the information you are given. You have practised evaluating texts and sources.

REVIEW AND REFLECTION

	I have learned about …	I need more practice with …
Why evaluation skills are important		
Evaluating reasoning and evidence in different arguments and perspectives		
Recognising bias and vested interest		
Understanding some elements of credibility (reputation, expertise, experience, access to information)		
Evaluating written sources		
Understanding the potential impact of others' arguments, perspectives and credibility on my own perspective		

Research

In this chapter you will start building your research skills, thinking about how you would select a global issue that you would like to research and how to find relevant information about it. Research is an investigative study of resources and materials around a topic or issue that aims to reach new conclusions or recommend courses of action. Research begins with curiosity and fills gaps in knowledge and learning. Developing research skills will help you problem solve, improve your knowledge on the topic or issue you are researching, and develop independent learning skills.

While studying this chapter you will read some perspectives on the topic of Climate change, energy and resources and plan part of a project based on the topic of Water, food and agriculture. You will practise carrying out some searches online for information about the topics of Transport, travel and tourism, Digital world, and Environment, pollution and conservation. As the chapter progresses, you will further explore how to find relevant information and how to check whether your sources are useful and reliable. You will practise planning and conducting some primary research and you will keep a record of where you found information. You will also practise some strategies for writing down your findings and learn about how to write up a research report, including acknowledging the sources you have used. These activities will include material on additional topics such as Health and wellbeing and Education for all. At the end of the chapter you will showcase your skills by writing a short research report.

BEFORE YOU START

Before you start work on this chapter, take a few minutes to think about the skills you already have that could help you with researching information.

Listed below are some skills you will be working on in this chapter. Put them into order from the one you feel you need to learn most about when learning about research, to the one you already feel most confident about:

- planning and organising what steps to take for a research project

- managing lots of information

- deciding what is relevant information to include

- keeping a record of sources.

5.1 Choosing a topic, identifying an issue and formulating a research question

In this course you will have the chance to research information and perspectives about different topics that you are interested in. You can choose an important or interesting issue to research and write an individual report or essay about it. You might also do some research for a team project. (In this case, the team would divide up the research so that team members do their own individual research and then share their ideas with the rest of the team.)

Choosing a topic and an issue to research

When you are beginning research you should choose a topic that interests you. This will help keep you motivated during your research. Topics covered in Cambridge IGCSE and O Level Global Perspectives are very broad and do not specify any issues, so you will have to narrow down what you want to find out about. To help you focus on your research it is helpful to write down a few aims for your research to achieve that are linked to the issue that you choose. You learned about mind-maps in Chapter 2 and this could be a useful way of identifying a specific issue relating to the main topic.

Figure 5.1 shows a mind-map that you can use to help you identify an issue for research.

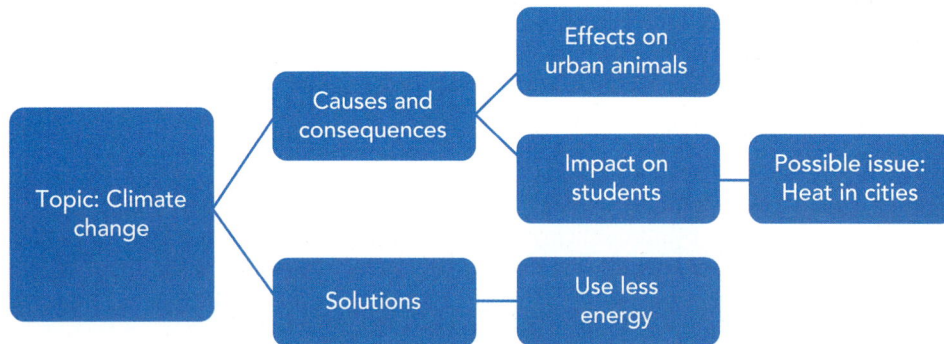

Figure 5.1: Mind-mapping can help identify an issue for research

Another way you could identify an issue to research is to do some reading about a topic you are interested in and find an issue in what you have read that you would like to find out more about. For example, you may be interested in inequality in the world and have read that there is a digital divide between countries and within communities. To decide if '*Digital inequality*' is an issue that you could research further you could ask:

- Is this issue getting worse over time?

- Are there multiple perspectives that can be researched?

- What are the main causes of this problem?

- What are the major consequences of this problem?

- What possible solutions are there to this problem?

Keep in mind the issue that you are addressing while you are researching. Be ready to change your issue if you cannot find enough information or perspectives that add to your research.

> **TIP**
>
> When you research an issue, you will be exploring global, national, local and personal perspectives. You may want to look back to Chapter 1 to remind yourself about these.

ACTIVITY 5.01

1   Read the text below, which is relevant to the topics of Climate change, energy and resources and Water, food and agriculture.

CONTINUED

Why fresh water shortages will cause the next great global crisis

Unfortunately for our planet, water supplies are now running dry at an alarming rate. The world's population continues to grow but that rise in numbers has not been matched by a similar increase in supplies of fresh water. Across the globe, reports reveal huge areas in crisis today as reservoirs and aquifers dry up. More than a billion individuals – one in seven people on the planet – do not have access to safe drinking water.

Last week in the Brazilian city of São Paulo, home to 20 million people, and once known as the City of Drizzle, drought got so bad that residents began drilling through basement floors and car parks to try to reach groundwater. City officials warned last week that they may have to ration water supplies. Citizens might have access to water for only two days a week, they added.

In California, officials have revealed that the state has entered its fourth year of drought with January this year becoming the driest since meteorological records began. At the same time, per capita water use has continued to rise.

In the Middle East, large areas of countryside have turned into desert because of overuse of water. Iran is one of the most severely affected. Heavy overconsumption of water, combined with poor rainfall, have severely reduced its water resources and its agricultural output. Similarly, the United Arab Emirates is so concerned about the lack of fresh water that it is now investing in desalination plants and wastewater treatment units.

The global nature of the crisis is underlined in similar reports from other regions. In south Asia, for example, there have been massive losses of groundwater, which has been pumped up for farming over the past decade. The area from eastern Pakistan, across the hot dry plains of northern India and into Bangladesh, is very densely populated. This is the most intensely irrigated land in the world. Up to 75% of farmers rely on pumped groundwater to water their crops. Water use is increasing – at the same time satellite images show that supplies are shrinking alarmingly.

Source: www.theguardian.com (2015, adapted)

2   Identify the issues and the perspectives in the passage above and put them under the correct heading in the table.

	Issues	Perspectives
1		
2		
3		

The text in Activity 5.01, written in 2015, might be useful for you to begin your research if you lived in Brazil and were researching the global issue of water shortages. You could then do further research on the Brazilian (national) perspective about water shortages. This could be compared with the perspective of people in São Paulo or your own hometown/local community.

These are some of the issues you may have identified and linked to these perspectives:

- population growth
- water supplies are running low
- reservoirs and aquifers are drying up
- no access to safe drinking water
- desertification in the Middle East (affecting environment)
- overuse of water
- low rainfall
- effect on agriculture
- need for desalination plants and wastewater treatment units
- loss of groundwater.

Similarly, you may have identified the following perspectives from the text:

- global
- local: Brazilian city of São Paolo (people who live there), California
- national: Middle East, Iran, South Asia, Pakistan, Bangladesh.

ACTIVITY 5.02

1   Read the following perspectives, which also focuses on the topic of Climate change, energy and resources and looks at the use of fossil fuels. As a challenge, you could get the whole class involved by creating a 'Thought Tunnel' and dividing the class into 3 groups representing the global, national and local perspectives. Using the text below, in your groups, discuss and add on to the perspectives so that everyone has something different to say about the same perspective. Two of the groups should line up opposite each other to provide contrasting viewpoints for the third group who will travel down the middle of the two lines listening to the different perspectives. The third group will then swap with one of the other groups and repeat the same process until everyone has heard the viewpoints twice. Then answer the question that follows. While you read, notice if the different perspectives agree with each other or if they disagree. You might identify an issue to research further by looking at different perspectives:

Global perspective	Globally, we know that climate change is a serious issue and that one of the reasons for this is the overuse of fossil fuels. We also know that the world's fossil fuels will run out soon if we continue to use them at the same rate as we are doing now. It is not sustainable to continue using fossil fuels. This is why we all need to find and use renewable sources of energy.

CONTINUED

National perspective	The government says, 'We cannot do anything about climate change as it is happening and will continue to happen regardless of whether we stop using fossil fuels or not.' The government also says, 'Our country needs to use fossil fuels to become as economically developed as other countries who have been using fossil fuels for years. It would be unfair if we could not catch up.'
Local perspective	Many people in your local community disagree with the national perspective given by the government. They think that because there is a lot of wind and sun in the area, there must be alternative ways of generating energy so that fossil fuels are not used for heating and lighting. They have seen how polluted some of the big cities are becoming and want to protect their local environment.

What are the possible issues you can identify from reading these perspectives?

2 Now consider your personal perspective. Do you agree with any of the three perspectives from the passage above?

You may not agree with any of them and have your own perspective and reasons for this. This is your personal perspective.

3 Write down your own perspective about fossil fuels and compare this with your partner's.

Did you both agree with the same perspective? Are your perspectives the same? If they are different, explain to each other why you think what you do.

Figure 5.2: Can we use less fossil fuel?

It is likely that, as you research global issues from different perspectives and find new information, your personal perspective will change. It is fine to change your own perspective; you just need to be sure that you have strong reasons for your personal perspective.

ACTIVITY 5.03

1   With a partner, or in a group, look at the table of perspectives below and decide for each one whether it is a global perspective (about the whole world or planet Earth), national perspective (about a particular country), local perspective (about the local area or community) or personal perspective, held by the speaker.

'Too many tourists cause problems for the local area. We do not have the infrastructure or space for them.'	'Tourists bring in a lot of money to the country. Their money and influence help us to develop.'
'Cities are not a good environment to live in.'	'It is really important that we provide good schools near to the areas where young people live, or provide buses for them to travel to school easily each day.'
'Young people have to move to the city to improve their prospects.'	'I cannot earn a living here if we don't get rain very soon.'
'We need to allow foreign people to come here to look after old people and work in hospitals.'	'We must build many more houses for the local population. We need land for that.'
'Young people spend too much time on the internet. They are becoming too westernised.'	'Modern lifestyles are not active enough. They damage people's health.'
'It makes no difference if I vote. The government is not interested in ordinary people.'	'If we want people to stay here, we have to provide better healthcare and look for new ideas about how to manage the local community.'
'Our rivers are polluted with chemicals and the fish are dying.'	'Politicians are corrupt. They want power and don't care about ordinary people.'
'People spend too much time on their mobile phones and don't interact properly with friends and family.'	'Mobile phones have boosted local business and made life easier for us.'

CONTINUED

2   Could any of these statements reflect more than one perspective? What issue or issues are they linked to? Copy down eight of the perspectives from this table and write down what you think the main issues could be. From your selection, choose one issue that you might like to research and write a few lines explaining your choice.

Searching for material on the internet

When you are thinking about what topic or issue you would like to research, you may want to start with some internet searches about the topic to see what sources of information are available. You might start your search with the title of the topic, for example Transport, travel and tourism. However, you may find that this is too broad and that you need to be more precise with your search terms. If this is the case, you will need to start narrowing down the question(s) you want to answer.

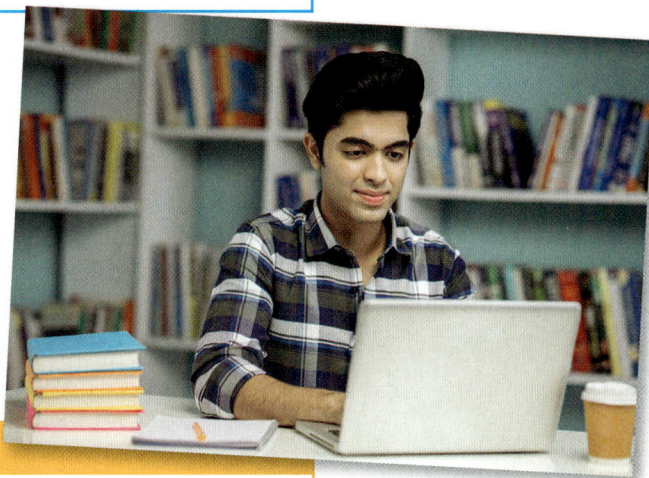

TIPS

- You will get too many results if you put only one or two words into a search engine. Put in between three and six key words to narrow your search.

- Put the main key word first: many search engines think this is the word you are looking for. Also, pay attention to the predictions that come before you type as this might give you further ideas.

- The main results always appear in order. Sometimes it might be worth looking beyond the first page, but it is probably more practical for you to change your search terms rather than look at all the results. More precise search terms mean you will find the information you need more quickly.

- Be aware of those results that are sponsored by commercial organisations (such as those labelled 'Ad', for advertisement). These may not be useful for your research as they are usually only interested in making money from those who visit their sites. Companies can also pay for their site to appear at the top of the list if certain terms are searched for, so the first few hits may not always be the most relevant ones.

ACTIVITY 5.04

While you carry out the activity below, make a few notes, because you will be discussing what you find afterwards.

1   Enter 'transport, travel and tourism' into your search engine. (You don't need to click on any of the websites on the results page, just look at the page of results you get.)

   a   How many results do you get? Quite a lot? Perhaps about two million: certainly too many for you to read!

CONTINUED

    b   What sort of sites do you get? You might have found that some of these are from organisations you have come across before and might use again, for example World Wildlife Fund (WWF) and World Health Organization (WHO); and there will definitely be a Wikipedia link.

2   Enter 'air travel' into the search engine. What sort of results do you get now? You should notice a change in the types of websites that are showing on the results page. You may find you get more results – why is this?

3   Now enter, 'restricting air travel' into the search engine. You might have noticed that as you refine your search, you are also creating a possible research question for your report or essay. What might your question be as a result of this activity? Do you notice any titles that include opinions or perspectives?

Figure 5.3: Should we restrict air travel?

4   Try this activity with another topic from the list that your teacher has suggested.

5   Find someone in your class who searched for the same topic as you in the search term activity and compare your notes. Make a table on a piece of paper to do this. It should list the number of sources each of you found, and the web address, title and author of each. For each of the sources write down from your notes whether it contains facts, opinions or both, and how relevant it is to the issue you were looking for information on. Did one of you find more results, or better results? Why might that be?

Formulating a research question

A research question is used to guide your research. It is often stated as a question which allows you to investigate different perspectives and arguments around the question. A research question should be clearly worded and avoid anything that might be too broad. It needs to state what the global problem is and what topic the problem is connected to.

Here are two examples of poorly worded research questions:

How to stop mosquitos.	Will animals be affected by climate change?
• Is not clearly worded. • Does not allow different perspectives. • Does not allow for different arguments.	• Is not clearly worded – does not allow for different perspectives or arguments. • Not specific enough – which animals are affected and by what part of climate change?

Now look at two examples of strong research questions:

Should free public transport for all be considered to help solve world pollution problems?	Can increasing eco-tourism help towards long-term conservation of the land and endangered animals?
• The question format allows for different perspectives. • Clearly states what the problem is and what issue they would like to investigate. • Will have lots of opportunities to research from different sources.	• Clearly states what the problem is and what is being investigated. • Opportunity to investigate different sources – perhaps compare case studies. • Opportunity to change the question – perhaps removing 'endangered animals' to focus more on the effects on the land.

Getting the research question right might take some time and changes.

5.2 Planning your research

When you have decided on the issue you would like to research, it is really important that you plan your research so that you keep focused on what you are looking for and do not become distracted by lots of interesting material that is not on topic.

Firstly, you will need to decide what you would like to find out about and how you will go about researching it.

ACTIVITY 5.05

Imagine the following situation.

You are working in a team, and the team has decided to do a project on the topic of Water, food and agriculture.

After some initial discussion and looking back at some of the work you have been doing in class about this topic, you decide to focus on the issue of food waste as a solution to food poverty. You want to find out how different countries are dealing with the issue of food poverty and what they do with food waste. You will use secondary research data about other countries collected from the internet. You should also do some primary research to find out what the situation is in your community and what different people think or know about food waste in the community.

You have decided to put together a short video clip to show to an audience. You hope to use the video as a way of persuading people to produce less food waste, and to donate money or items of food (tins, packets, etc.) to a food bank in your community.

Figure 5.4: Food inequality is a major global issue

1   Consider:

   a   What information do you think you need to find out about food waste and people's different perspectives?

   b   How are you going to find out this information?

2   Draw a flow chart or mind-map to show your ideas.

3   Share your ideas with a partner. You can do this by comparing your diagrams to identify their similarities and differences. Create a larger diagram which combines your ideas including all the information you have both found and all of the different ways of finding it.

Once you have a good idea of what you would like to find out and how you will go about this, it is a good idea to draw up a research plan, in which you outline:

- the topic and issue you will be researching
- the aim(s) of your project
- what you would like to find out and what methods you will use
- what sources of information you will investigate
- how you will organise/record your findings
- what problems you might encounter and how you will solve them.

Here is an example of a research plan that someone wrote after they had decided on an issue to discuss in an individual research report. (Notice that this is not an essay plan; it is a plan of how someone might research their question.)

1	Question/ topic	Should genetically modified (GM) crops be used to help solve world food shortages?
2	Research aims	The research is about the perspectives (global, national, local including relevant people such as scientists, politicians, etc.) about GM foods and how important they are for food security around the world.
		The idea is to find out if GM foods are a real solution to the problem of food shortages.
3	Issue	The issue that I am researching is world food shortages. I know that there is food inequality in the world.
		I think most people in the West have enough food but many people in developing countries do not.
		It is often shown in the media that people are dying of hunger in some parts of the world.
4	Methods	I can use the internet to find out global and national perspectives. My teacher has given me a list of useful websites I could explore.
		I can do interviews and talk with people in my community and in school to see what they think about the issue – this will give me the local perspective. Interviews are good as primary research because you can tell what people really think and ask extra questions.
5	Sources of data and evidence	The internet is the easiest for secondary research. I will search for newspaper articles and video clips, or look at websites such as the United Nations or the World Economic Forum to get information from different perspectives.
		I need to find out if my ideas about food inequality are true and also if there is information to support what different people or organisations think about it. I will need numerical data to support these ideas.
		I can interview people in school: teachers as well as students. I can also organise interviews with doctors at my local hospital and with members of any local charities. They will give me evidence that I can use as primary sources. I can also look for trends and differences in what they say.

6 Recording of data and evidence	I will copy important information from the internet. I might make notes or summarise. I will copy the internet addresses and names of authors and the date I found them, so that I can remember where I found the information.
	What people say will be written down in notes, but I might try to save the interviews to listen to them again and compare with others.
	Some people might not like being recorded, so I will ask for permission and I will explain that I will just summarise what they say for my report and then delete the interview from my phone.
	If they are not happy with that, I can write notes next to questions to give me some ideas of what they said.
7 Possible problems	I might not get enough people to interview for the local perspective.
	I don't know if it is OK to record the answers, but if I ask them for permission, they may not tell the truth. Some people may not tell the truth anyway. They could be biased or just make fun of my work.
	I might not be able to find information or different perspectives. If that happens, I will need to change my question or maybe look for a different issue. While I am looking for information and perspectives, I might find something that people do not agree about, and change my focus to that, changing my question so that it is easier to answer.

DISCUSSION

Look at the research plan above. With a partner, discuss the following questions:

1   Is it clear what the report will be about?

2   Does this person understand the problems that might come up?

3   Is there anything else the author might have included?

Be ready to discuss your ideas in class.

When you have produced your overall research plan, you should consider what actions you will need to take to carry it out. You can then produce an action plan, which should include details of how you will manage your time and activities ready for writing your report.

ACTIVITY 5.06

1   Read the following two example extracts from action plans for
    individual reports. Give two strengths and one weakness of each.

Example 1

Name: Hans

Question: Can reducing greenhouse gas emissions globally help towards **sustainable living**?

KEY TASK	ACTIONS	ESTIMATE OF TIME NEEDED	DATE FOR COMPLETION
1 Get approval for report title.	Draft title based on topic.	30 minutes	2 Sept
	List reasons for choice of topic and question.	1 hour	2 Sept
	Identify possible problems in doing the research.	15 minutes	3 Sept for 4 Sept
	Make appointment with teacher to finalise title.	5 minutes plus 15-minute consultation	2 Sept
2 Identify local, national and global perspectives and research relevant sources using internet.	Book access to library computers for next two lunchtimes and check availability at home to shared family PC.	10 minutes	3 Sept
	Discuss perspectives and issues with teacher.	15 minutes	4 Sept
	Plan research.	15 minutes	4 Sept
	Do research.	??	??

KEY TERM

sustainable living: a lifestyle that attempts to reduce an individual's or society's use of the Earth's natural resources and personal resources.

CONTINUED

Example 2

Name: Joanna

Question: Does urbanisation worldwide have a bad impact on sustainable living?

Key task	Actions	Estimate of time needed	Date for completion
1 Get approval	See teacher as soon as possible.		
2 Start research	Use tablet at home.	4 days	Next month
	Use computer room at school.	4 days	Next month

2   Discuss the strengths and weaknesses of these two action plans with a partner. What might you tell each person if you were the teacher reviewing these action plans? What would you add to each of the action plans to improve them? Choose one of the action plans above and rewrite it to make it more useful.

5.3 Finding relevant information

One important research skill is how to select relevant information. You will need to narrow down what you look for and decide the limits for your research. If you do not narrow your focus, you could end up getting lost in all the information and different perspectives you might find on the internet, in newspapers, books and elsewhere. If you have too much information, it can be too much to manage.

You might do most of your research online, but you can also visit the library, or find out information by interviewing people or asking them to fill in a questionnaire. Interviewing people is a good way of finding out what different people think or feel about things, but you might not be able to trust the information you get from them. You can also research by observing what is going on around you, making notes of what you see. When you find out information and ideas directly by asking people, or collecting information by observation, this is called primary research. When you find out information from online sources or books, this is called secondary research.

DISCUSSION

How do you think you could focus your search for information and perspectives? How can you avoid collecting material/ reading information that is not relevant for your own needs?

Note down your thoughts.

Share your ideas with your partner. Make a note of any good ideas your partner shares.

ACTIVITY 5.07

1   Think about this question, which could be researched and answered in a research report or essay: *'Should air travel be restricted?'*

This is quite a broad question. If you were going to research this, what sort of information would you look for?

2   Write down five questions you might need to find answers for.

3   Discuss your five questions about air travel with a partner. Do they have the same ideas? Could you make the question more focused?

4   Amend the question if you think you could improve it.

Selecting sources of information

Figure 5.5: Information can come from a variety of sources

When you are working on your team project or individual report, you will need to find information from a variety of different sources and combine it together (Figure 5.5). Sometimes this information might be **primary data** which you collect directly yourself, such as personal observations you make or responses to questionnaires or surveys you design and distribute. A **primary source** of information can be very useful for research as it provides information from people who have a direct connection to the issue or topic. Some examples of primary sources include: letters, diaries, interviews, autobiographies, photographs, audio and video recordings, as well as artefacts and objects. Using primary sources and data can give you a first-hand opinion from people who are or were directly involved at the time.

KEY TERMS

primary data: information collected directly, for example through questionnaires, surveys or interviews.

primary source: an original document or object giving an account of the event or topic being researched.

In other cases, the information you collect might be **secondary data**, from a **secondary source**, which is information that has been published and may contain primary data which has already been analysed by someone else. Some examples of secondary sources are: textbooks, histories, biographies, government reports, encyclopaedias and documentaries. Secondary sources and data come in useful when you need to make use of a wider range of evidence which has been collected and analysed by someone else who may have relevant expertise on the topic you are researching, such as online charity organisations and government agencies.

Both primary and secondary sources of information can benefit your research, but they do have limitations. Some sources have more credibility than others. Some sources are more accurate than others. All sources can interpreted in different ways.

KEY TERMS

secondary data: information from published sources on the internet, in newspapers, magazines, journals or books.

secondary source: gives information about a primary source. This information may cover the same topic but has been collected and arranged from a number of different sources.

TIP

When identifying potentially useful sources, keep your research topic or question in mind so that you can select sources only if they are really relevant and are providing information or perspectives on the issue you are researching.

Of course you can keep a note of other interesting material to look at later, or in case you actually change your mind about the issue or question you are going to research. You should make this decision early on, to avoid too much wasted time researching material you are not going to use.

ACTIVITY 5.08

With a partner look at the list of topics and issues below and then the list of people/organisations provided. Decide which people/organisations would be useful sources of information or views on each topic. Might some of them be useful for more than one topic?

Could you think of anyone else/any other organisations that could provide useful information?

Discuss and be ready to share your reasoning with others. If you are unsure about any of the words, ask your teacher to explain.

Tourism	Climate change	Sport
Water & food	Education for all	Trade & aid
Employment	Migration	Health
Pollution	Social media	Values & beliefs

CONTINUED

The United Nations	A teenager	Minister for Agriculture
Someone who lives in Dubai	The president of a country	The head of FIFA
A hotel owner	Someone who works for UNICEF	A lawyer
A doctor (medical)	Greenpeace	A student
A coach	A farmer	Climate Action Network
A parent	A shopkeeper	World Vegetable Center

ACTIVITY 5.09

1   What sources of information might you use to find answers to the five questions you wrote down in Activity 5.07? List the secondary sources you think you might use. Would you also collect some primary data?

2   Write a note about each source explaining how it might help you to answer your questions and which question each might answer.

3   Share your notes on a display board (this can be a physical one or an electronic slide, or similar). If you are doing this activity with others then they can also share their notes on the board.

4   Look at the board and discuss what it tells you about the types of sources you would like to make use of for research in the future.

Verifying your sources

When selecting the sources you are going to use in a research project, it is important to check that they are providing accurate information. One way of checking this is to check them against other sources to see if they agree. This is called **verifying**.

Often you will be able to check whether or not information is correct as it will appear in different types of sources that can be classed as credible and reliable, for example international organisations, charity websites and articles from international news sources. If you can only find information in sites that can be edited by anyone, such as Wikipedia, you need to be careful – they may not be reliable. Many blogs are reliable, but you should always check on the author; some are experts and trustworthy, others are just individuals giving unsupported opinions or theories. Personal opinions can be

KEY TERM

verifying: making sure that something is true, accurate or justified.

used in research, but you need to be able to provide support for your ideas by finding credible, verified sources that also share the same view.

Figure 5.6: Unsupported opinions cannot be verified

When assessing whether a source is accurate and useful for a research project, you should apply the skills of analysis and evaluation that you developed in Chapters 3 and 4. To help you evaluate a source to see how useful it would be for your research, look carefully at the first table below. It shows a range of features you could think about when you are deciding if your sources are useful and reliable.

Is it accurate?	Make sure any evidence provided is true and correct and that any data presented is exact and believable. Check that there are no obvious mistakes; even spelling mistakes can indicate a problem with a site!
Is it credible?	Make sure that the writer knows about the issue and has access to information about it.
	Can you trust the source? Does the writer have a good reputation or expertise or experience?
Is it neutral/ objective?	Make sure there is no bias or vested interest in the source.
	Could there be any reason the source might provide incorrect information or try to mislead the reader?
Is it up to date?	Check when the source was published or written. What dates does it give for any figures or evidence it provides?
	Would this be a problem for the topic you are researching?
Is it relevant?	Make sure the source actually provides information or perspectives about the issue you are researching.

ACTIVITY 5.10

Practise verifying (checking information about) online sources, as follows:

1   Search for 'endangered species, wild tigers', which relates to the global topic of Environment, pollution and conservation, to find a source that tells you about the current situation of wild tigers.

2   Copy and paste any facts you find out about wild tigers into your search engine to find other sources that have the same information.

3   Make a note of the sources you found which had the same information. Did you find more than one source of information with the same details for this activity?

4   Share your findings with a partner. Explain to each other which sources you found that you think are reliable and why.

Selecting sources for a research report or essay

When selecting sources of information to use in an individual research report, you may find the diagram shown in Figure 5.7 helpful.

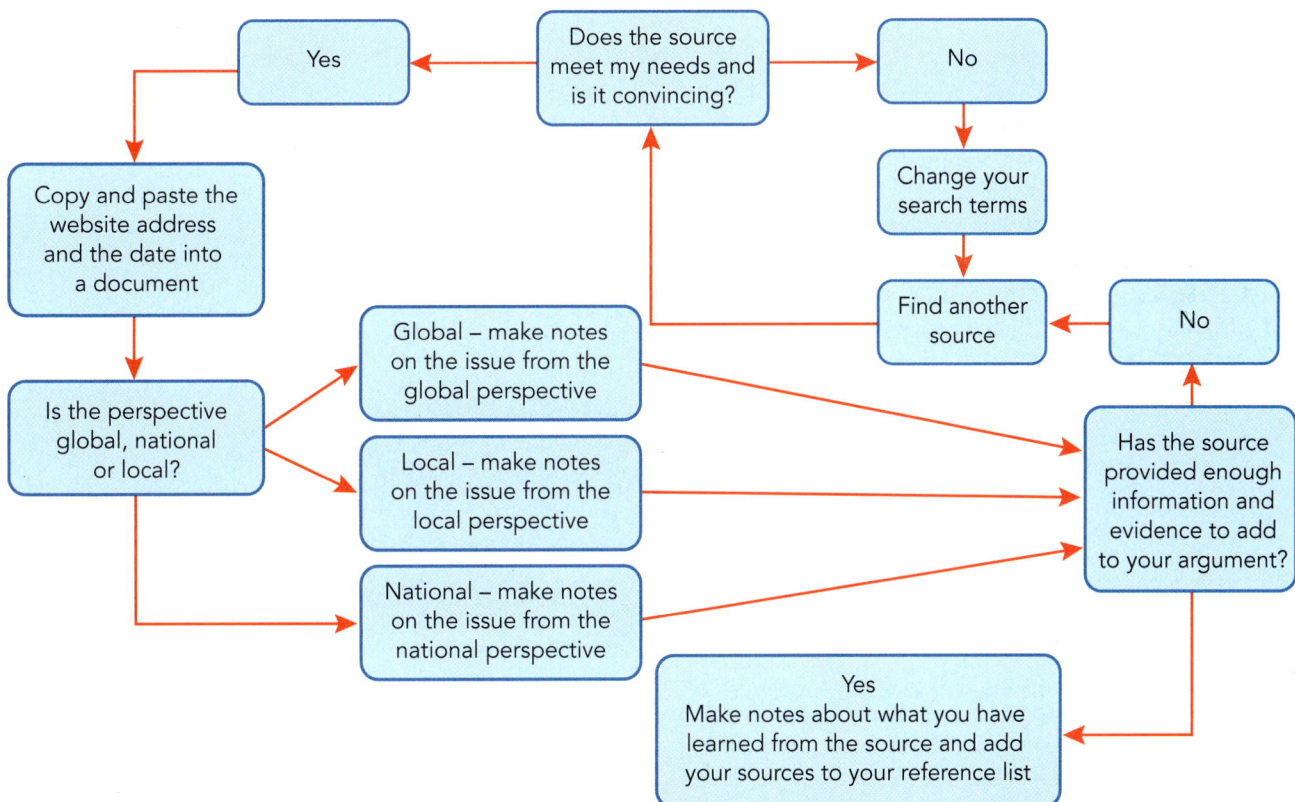

Figure 5.7: Source selection for an individual research report

---

ACTIVITY 5.11

Imagine you have been doing some research on a question for an individual research report relating to the topic Digital world. The research question is: *'Has the internet changed the world for the better?'*

When searching for information, you come across three different websites:

a   a blog for and by people aged over 50 in the United Kingdom

b   a newspaper article dated four years ago

c   an article from a magazine about the impact of technology written in the current year.

1   With a partner discuss the following questions:

   a   Which of these three sources do you think might be the best for your research? Why?

   b   Which of these three sources do you think might be unreliable? Why?

   c   Which of these three sources do you think is the most credible? Why?

2   Now, with your partner, think of a strength and a weakness of each of the three sources and write them down. Keep in mind what you are researching. You can use any of the information about sources and evaluation you have practised in the course so far. Be ready to share your thoughts with others.

5.4 Conducting your research

Whether you decide to decide to do mainly primary research, mainly secondary research or a mixture of both, you will need to decide on the **research methods** you are going to use to collect information.

Primary research

The most common primary research method is simply to ask people what they think about an issue. To do this effectively, you will need to think about what information you need and who you need to ask. The information you get will help you to understand whether the aim of your project is achievable and if any proposed course of action you carry out as a team will work. One way of planning your primary research is to draw a flow chart showing the perspectives you want to explore, the questions you want to ask and the places you might go to ask these questions. From your flow chart, you can focus in on the questions you might want to ask. Decide from where you might find out the information you need and who you are going to approach.

> **KEY TERM**
>
> **research methods:** the methods used to gather data and information that will be used in your work to support the points you make.

Figure 5.8 provides an example of a flow chart researching food waste.

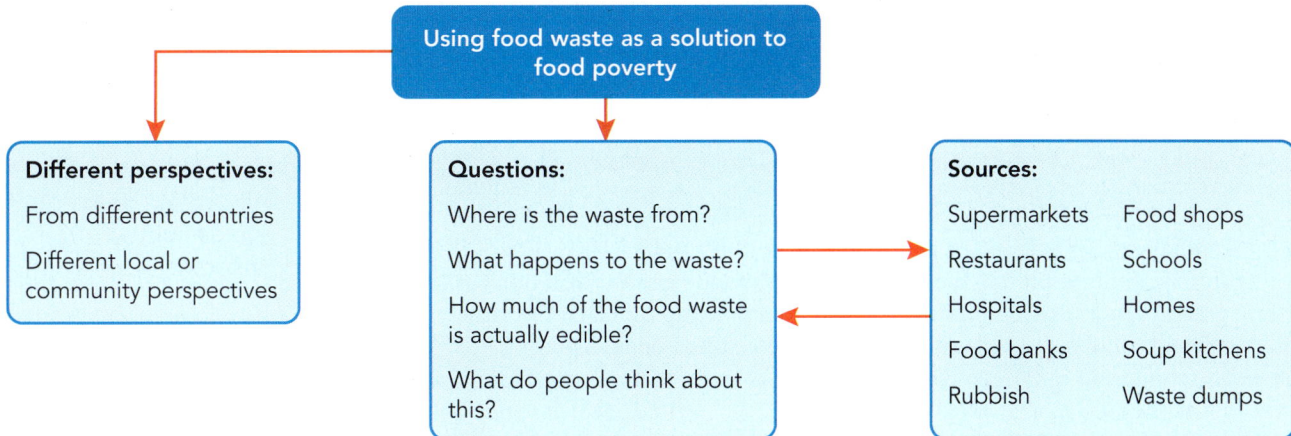

Using food waste as a solution to food poverty

Different perspectives:

From different countries

Different local or community perspectives

Questions:

Where is the waste from?

What happens to the waste?

How much of the food waste is actually edible?

What do people think about this?

Sources:

Supermarkets	Food shops
Restaurants	Schools
Hospitals	Homes
Food banks	Soup kitchens
Rubbish	Waste dumps

Figure 5.8: Food waste research flow chart

The example flow chart suggests that you could speak to a range of people working in different places, including supermarkets or food shops. You want their perspective about how much edible food is thrown away, and what they think might be done with it instead. You might also want the perspective of people who work for a charity, such as a food bank or soup kitchen; they may be able to tell you their thoughts about food poverty and where they get their food from. For another perspective, to find out what other countries do with food waste, you could look for contacts abroad who might be willing to complete your emailed questionnaire.

> **TIP**
>
> You might want to use primary research when writing an individual report or essay to find out about the local perspective on an issue.

Figure 5.9: Could using food waste be a solution to poverty?

Questionnaires, surveys and interviews

You can ask people for their views in a number of ways. Common research methods for primary research are

- questionnaires and surveys
- interviews.

Research conducted by a **questionnaire** asks a set of questions of an individual and collects the information on how they respond. The questions asked are usually short and do not give respondents the ability to explain their answer. A **survey** is the process of analysing and interpreting the information collected from the questions asked. Survey results can be used in different ways, from noticing trends in the answers to the questions, to selecting a specific age group or gender and interpreting how they respond to different questions. There are benefits in conducting a questionnaire in your research as they are easy to give out and can be given digitally, which means you can send it to a wider group of people.

Interviews are used in research to collect in-depth information or experiences from people. They are usually conducted orally, with the interviewer asking questions and the person being interviewed responding verbally. Interviews allow people to explain themselves in detail and take much more time to complete than a questionnaire. Consequently interviews are usually conducted with experts, witnesses or people with first-hand knowledge of a topic or issue.

> ### KEY TERMS
>
> **questionnaire:** a set of written questions with choice of answers that can be used to collect information from a large number of people.
>
> **survey:** a research method used to collect data from specific set of people to gain insights and information on a topic.
>
> **interview:** a meeting where a researcher can obtain information by asking questions.

ACTIVITY 5.12

Part 1

Imagine you want to do some primary research to find out what motivates different people, what they think about work, why they work and how important motivation is for them to do a good job. The aim of the activity will be to produce a digital presentation of your research findings using graphs or tables to show the results. You will aim to persuade people that being well motivated leads to better performance at work. Answer the following questions:

1 Who are you going to ask?

2 How many people are you going to ask?

3 What information do you want?

4 What methods are you going to use?

5 How are you going to collect information?

6 How are you going to record information?

7 What are you going to do with the information you collect?

Discuss your ideas with a partner.

Part 2

For this part of the activity, you are going to conduct some primary research. Limit the number of people you are going to ask to ten. They should be people at your school (learners, teachers and other school staff), parents and relatives and/or neighbours.

CONTINUED

You will ask them to complete a questionnaire with ten questions about what motivates them, what they think about work, why they work and how important motivation is for them to do a good job.

1   Work with your partner to design your questionnaire.

2   Ask your teacher for feedback so that you can improve your questionnaire.

3   Each of you should hand your questionnaire to the ten people you have chosen (total 20).

4   Collect your questionnaires (after about one week; you will need to tell your respondents this when you hand them out).

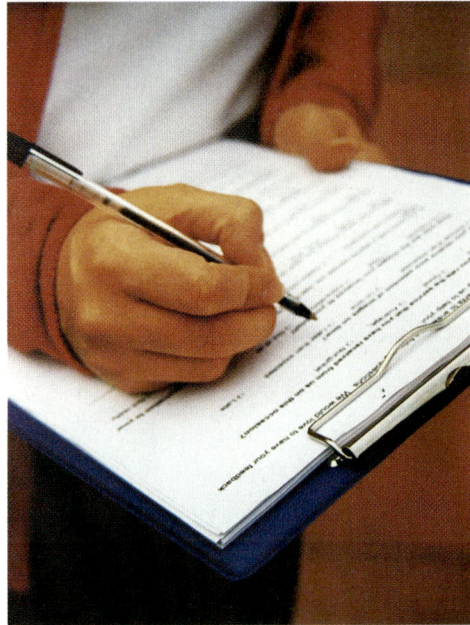

Figure 5.10: Questionnaires can be used for primary research

5   Analyse the information you have gathered by looking at the results. How many people answered? How many gave the same or similar answers and what did they say?

6   Design a digital presentation to persuade people that being well motivated leads to better performance at work. (You can work together on the presentation, combining all the information you collected, or you can work individually and only use your own findings from the ten people you surveyed.)

7   Ask your teacher to give you feedback on your graphs or tables showing your findings – does it show your primary research findings in a clear way? Does it persuade your teacher?

Ethical considerations

When you do primary research, collecting data from people directly, it is important to consider **ethics**. By this, we mean rules and ideas which help us to understand the right thing to do in specific situations. For example, when you interview people it is important that you behave in a way that does not cause any harm to them. Also, you must treat all the information you gather as confidential. You must get permission from the interviewee to ask them questions and use their answers in your work.

You can anonymise the names of your interviewees, so there is no need to use their real names. It is enough to get information, showing different perspectives on the issue, to include in your reflection on the project. You can provide a note of where and when you interviewed or surveyed people, rather than including actual names.

KEY TERM

ethics: principles of what is right and wrong, for example when conducting an activity like research.

5.5 Recording and organising your research

While you are conducting your research, you will need to record:

- the details of the research itself (in other words, how you have collected your information and the sources you have used)

- the information that you collected (for example the facts and perspectives that you have gathered from your primary research or from the secondary sources that you have used). This will form the basis of your report or essay.

You will be managing a lot of information, so it will help if you organise it efficiently.

Recording your research

As you saw in Activity 5.04, each time you type a different term into the search engine, you get different results. If you do not keep a record of where you look and which search terms you used, you can waste a lot of time, repeating the same search or not being able to find useful sources.

Record each source you use in your research and any useful links you find. It is helpful to copy website links and keep them in a document with a note about how useful they are to save you time when you have decided exactly what you are going to research about and which perspectives you are going to present. This is called a source recording sheet.

When you use other people's work, you should be honest about this. You must keep a record of the name of the publication you have used, the author, its date of publication and where you found it (in other words the book or magazine, or web address if it was from the internet). This means you will be able to make a list of references to go with your work. This list will show whose work you have made use of and allow your readers to find it themselves so they can compare or follow up on your research.

Sometimes we find sources that do not seem very trustworthy or reliable, but they give us a useful point of view, or a different perspective on an issue. So we use their ideas, but we keep a note that they might be unreliable.

After completing an individual or a team research project, you should be able to say whether sources were useful or not, what you learned from them and whether you felt that you could trust them. You have learned about evaluating sources in Chapter 4; for the purpose of your resource record you can decide if the sources are useful or not by providing a quick 'star' rating on your reference sheet. 1 star means the source is not very useful and 5 stars means that the source is very useful to your research (Figure 5.11).

Ref	Author	Year	Title	Reference type	Notes	Rating
1	Jones, G.	2021	Research techniques	Book (I used pages 78–89)	Useful for creating surveys	***
2	United Nations	2022	"Library"	Website: https://research. un.org/en/un- resources/topic	Lots of good secondary information	*****

Figure 5.11: Example of a source recording sheet with ratings

---

ACTIVITY 5.13

1 With a partner, or on your own, choose a topic to research. It could be one of the topics you have already looked at.

2 If you are working with a partner, agree an area of research and maybe a specific issue, and then decide on some search terms.

3 Type your search terms into your search engine.

4 You may find that the links are not directly relevant to what you are looking for. If this is the case then ignore them and move on to the next result. It may be however that they are partly relevant but suggest a way in which you should refocus your research by changing your search terms. If this happens, make a note of the other issues they are considering before you move on.

  You may change your mind about what you want to research. If you find another interesting issue you can note down interesting links in a separate list. If you have already decided, ignore any links that are about a different issue.

5 Choose one link and click on it.

6 When the page opens, skim the information and decide if the page or article is relevant to your research. If it is, copy and paste the full web address into your source reference sheet.

  On your document, make a note of the name of the website and the author. Make a note of the title of the article or webpage.

  If there is a date on the article or page showing when it was written or created, note that as well. If there is no date, type ND. This can help you decide if the information is current.

CONTINUED

Click on 'About' or 'About us' to find out information about the website and try to find out about the author. Sometimes you can do this by clicking on the author's name, or their picture, or there may be a short piece of information called 'About the author'. Is the author an expert? Do you think the source is credible?

Write one sentence summarising what the author has written. Follow it with a sentence on whether you think this source would be useful to your research.

7 Repeat steps 5 and 6 with two or three more links.

8 Save your document as 'Research on ...' (the topic/issue you are looking for).

REFLECTION

Why should you keep a record of your sources of information and perspectives?

Write down your ideas.

Recording your findings

Whether you are doing primary or secondary research, it is important to develop strong skills for taking notes. When interviewing people about their opinions you will need to note down what they say; when analysing the results of questionnaires you will have to take notes of your findings; and when you are researching online or in books, newspapers or magazines, you will need to take notes about the content of the sources you are reading, including any facts, opinions or perspectives that you found in them, and how these relate to other sources you have read.

Notes are lists of words or phrases written down to help us remember. Key words can bring back memories. For example, think of the word 'dentist'. What comes to mind? Notes should be short and clear. One word can help us to remember other details. Notes will help to remind you of what you have read and where you found information and sources. This will save you time and worry. Without organised notes, you may end up re-reading the same sources and confusing yourself.

We can write notes before we do something, to make sure we don't forget to do everything we intend to do. We can also take notes while we are doing something. Note-taking is a useful skill because, as we saw in the section about memory, it is not possible for us to remember everything we do, see and hear. We need to choose the important facts and keep a record to help us remember.

We can write notes while we are listening or watching or discussing, so that we can look at our main points afterwards. This helps us to remember other details. And, of course, we can write things down afterwards that might be useful to us later on in our research.

ACTIVITY 5.14

Find a short film clip or a video showing an event that interests you. For example, you might look for a clip called the 'Invisible Gorilla Test'. While you listen or watch, write down a few key words to remind you of what you see.

If you do choose the 'Invisible Gorilla Test' clip, without giving too much away, you might benefit from watching it first without taking any notes. For the second viewing, write down key words to remind you of what you saw. By doing this you may notice more than you did on the first viewing.

Notes are very useful for studying. At school we can take notes on important things our teachers say. At university, we will take notes while we listen to, or watch, lectures.

Because we only write down occasional words or phrases, this allows us to listen carefully. If we try to write everything down, we concentrate on trying to write instead of listening carefully. This can happen in a **dictation** exercise, when a teacher reads text aloud and we write down exactly what the teacher reads out. Then we can find it very difficult to absorb what is being said, even though we have written it down.

You will find note-taking especially useful when writing a research report or doing research for an essay or another piece of written work. You will need to note down useful information or ideas you read so that you can write your report or essay in your own words, sometimes quoting from sources you have found. If you note where you found quotations that you want to use, this will make your life easier when you actually write your essay. You can arrange your notes so that you keep information about different perspectives together and examples and evidence organised. Then when you plan your essay, you have a clear idea of what you might write and any more research you might need to do.

KEY TERM

dictation: saying something aloud for someone else to write down in order to create a record of it.

REFLECTION

Think about writing notes. Have you ever written notes yourself, or seen someone else take notes? When? Where? Why? Did you find them useful? In what ways did they help?

Deciding what to write down

We've seen that when we make notes, we just write down key words or phrases. We do not try to write down everything we see or every word we hear.

So how do we work out which words or phrases are key and will help us to remember more of what we do, see or hear?

The first step is to understand what we need to remember. The way we decide is by being selective. We have to plan a bit in advance so that we choose the right things to write down.

In class we are sometimes given questions to answer while we listen to a recording, watch a clip, or read a text. While we listen, watch or read, we note down details that are relevant to the questions. This helps us to select the important points.

TIP

When you are working in a team on a project, it is sensible to make notes of your own research findings and the sources you looked at, and then to keep a log of what happens, things that go well, any challenges or difficulties you experience. If you write these down when they happen, or soon after, this will make it much easier to write a clear reflection afterwards.

When we are not given questions, we need to come up with our own and either write them down and leave space for the notes, or try to keep them in mind while we listen, watch or read. You may have had some experience of this in your Science classes if you have done any practical work. You have some questions or a worksheet to complete while the experiment is going on and maybe a question to answer at the end. This helps you to remember.

ACTIVITY 5.15

The text below is on the subject of the eating habits of teenagers. While you are reading, note down the answers to the following questions. Just write words or phrases, not full sentences. Try to read the text once only.

1   Who were the subjects of the study?

2   Why was the study done?

3   What was the study about?

4   Why is it important to eat fruit and vegetables?

5   Why is fast food unhealthy?

Some worrying news about the eating habits of teenagers in the USA

A recent study conducted in the USA has found that more than two-thirds of all teenagers drink sweet fizzy drinks like lemonade every day and that almost half of all those asked eat fast food daily. In contrast to this, many teenagers do not eat enough fruit and vegetables. Less than a quarter of those asked ate five portions of fruit and vegetables per day, which is the recommended amount. Fruit and vegetables are low in calories and high in fibre, vitamins and minerals, so according to researchers, eating a diet high in fruit and vegetables helps to prevent health problems such as diabetes, heart disease and cancer. On the other hand, fast foods are high in fat and calories. Consuming fast food and fizzy drinks increases the number of calories teenagers eat which, without increased activity, can cause obesity, which leads to disease.

Researchers say that one aim of the study was to provide information to those people responsible for creating health policy. For example, the findings about fizzy drinks and fast food may help policymakers decide whether to ban sales of these items on school campuses.

Figure 5.12: A study of teenage eating habits showed a worrying trend

---

Ways of taking notes

There are many ways to take notes effectively. You could:

- Use colour (for example, red for questions, blue for conclusions, green for supporting information). Using a colour code helps you to find what you are looking for later on. If you always use the same colour, or picture, or symbol, for each type of note, you can **scan** several pages quickly and easily find the one type of note you are looking for.

- Create diagrams – or add labels to existing diagrams.

- Include visual aids.

One effective way to create notes is to write short summaries of what you found interesting. When reading a source for your research, write a summary of what you read in your own words. This will make your workload more manageable because it will reduce the amount of material you have to work with when you come to write up your research.

When writing summaries, keep the following guidelines in mind:

1 Do not copy the original piece.

2 Keep your summary short – aim for approximately 100 words, depending on the text you are summarising.

3 Use your own words.

4 Read the original piece with the questions: Who? What? When? Where? Why? How? in mind and put the answers in your summary.

5 Describe the main ideas of the original piece.

6 Do not include your opinion of the issue or topic discussed in the original piece.

KEY TERM

scan: to look quickly at a text, without reading it, to find certain details.

ACTIVITY 5.16

1 Read the summary below and answer the questions that follow.

Sustainable living in Bradinton

In 2022, Bradinton became an energy efficient community. Solar panels have now been installed on the roofs of all the houses. These panels capture energy from the sun and convert it into electricity for powering home appliances like computers, televisions, and refrigerators. Solar power also provides heating and hot water for the houses. This use of solar power reduces everyone's dependence on energy sources such as oil and gas, which are harmful to the environment. Bradinton has become an environmentally aware community. Bradinton can be used as an example for other communities that want to move towards a sustainable future.

CONTINUED

   a   How many words does the summary contain?

   b   Does the summary give you information to answer the questions: who? what? when? where? why? and how?

   c   Does the summary contain any opinion?

   d   Do you think summary writing will help you to manage your research material and to build up your individual report?

2   Form a group of 3–4. Discuss what sustainable living means to your group. Create a mood board (either digitally or drawn/collaged) that represent who, what, when, where, why, how. Display or showcase your designs and explain it to another group in your class.

Organising your findings

As you take notes of your plans, of the information you find out about your topic, about perspectives and about sources, you will find you have a lot of material. You need to keep notes somewhere to tell you what you have found in the sources you think you might use: a few details about each source and what you might use the material for. If you have the details of the source recorded, you can always return to it later to find more information, or to check that your notes are accurate.

If you are researching different topics for your team project and your individual report, you will need to keep your research separate for each.

There are many ways of organising material. It is easy enough to keep copies of your documents with notes of websites and other details on your computer, the cloud, a memory stick or other portable storage. But you do need to make sure you label and organise your documents and files from the beginning. So you must plan how you will organise your research material before you have collected too much to manage.

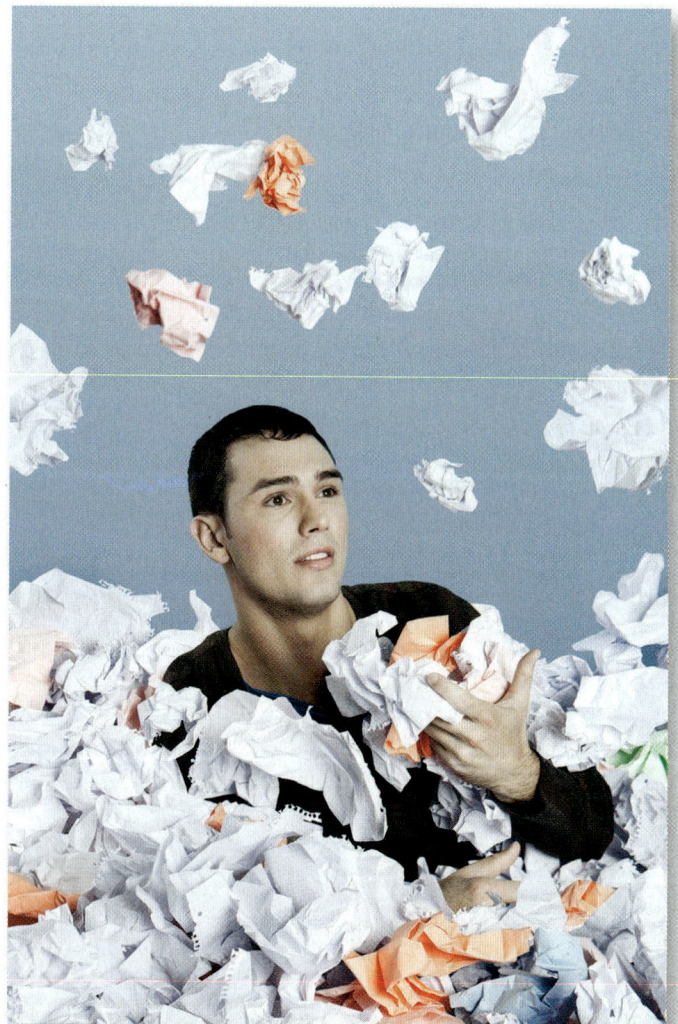

Figure 5.13: Organise!

5.6 Writing a research report

When writing up your research into a report or essay, you will need to pace yourself and give yourself enough time to complete each stage of the writing process. You should consider how much time you have to do the writing and create a timeframe to complete your report. You should follow these stages when writing a research report:

- write your first draft
- revise (re-read and make changes)
- write your final draft
- ensure your report is within any word limit you have been given
- create a reference list
- proofread (check and correct).

If you have taken good notes during your research, and have been using them to write up summaries and paragraphs while working and exploring issues within lessons, you will find writing your report should be straightforward.

Acknowledging other people's ideas

When you use other people's words or ideas, you should make sure you credit them and do not give the impression that the information and ideas are all your own.

DISCUSSION

How would you feel if someone took your work secretly and copied it and then handed it in to the teacher as their own work?

How would you feel if your friend was struggling with some work; they came to you and asked for help, discussed ideas with you and then wrote their own work afterwards and told the teacher that you had helped?

Would you feel differently about these two experiences? Why?

Discuss your ideas with your partner.

Copying someone else's words or phrases, even if you did not mean to do so, is called plagiarism. Plagiarism is a very serious issue and if a researcher's work is discovered to be plagiarised, the researcher can lose their reputation, in addition to breaking copyright laws. These are laws which protect authors' rights over their own work, so others cannot make use of it without their permission.

TIP

Writing clearly is an important communication skill. Chapter 6 will help you develop strong communication skills, including improving your writing.

KEY TERMS

revise: to re-read a text and make changes (in content, organisation, sentence structures, and word choice) to improve it. During revision, you may want to add, remove, move and/or substitute text.

proofread: the last thing you do before declaring a piece of written work is 'finished'. Pay attention to your grammar. Correct all the spelling errors, especially the ones that spell-checking misses (such as 'there'/'their', and 'to'/'too').

plagiarism: intentionally or unintentionally copying the words and phrases of someone else and presenting them as your own work.

copyright: a law that gives the owner of a written document, music, book or picture the right to decide what can be done with it. If work is copyrighted, it can only be copied with permission from the author.

Citing

When you quote an author or use their ideas you must credit the author or state the publication that the information came from. This is called **citing**. You need to cite the source of a quote or idea exactly at the point that you have used it in your writing.

It is possible that you might include some direct quotes, when you give the exact words written or spoken by a source. If you quote exact words, these should be in quotation marks, cited on the page and also listed on the reference sheet at the end of the report. Often it is best to include only a few quotes, as they are counted in the word count limit and are not considered to be your own work. Quotes are most appropriate for stated opinions that give evidence of perspectives for your report.

> Pollution and climate change go hand in hand. Across the planet, most of the electricity that humans use is still made by burning large amounts of fossil fuels. Renewable energy sources, such as solar and wind power emits hardly any pollutants into the atmosphere, but the changes needed to stop pollution entering the air are not happening fast enough. In fact, only '29 percent of electricity comes from renewable sources' (United Nations, 2022) at the moment, however many cities around the world have begun to respond to this problem and are investing in more renewable sources of energy.

Figure 5.14: Example of a citation

Referencing and creating a bibliography

You must reference all the sources you use in your work; this includes sources you have cited. There are many different forms of referencing. It does not matter which form of referencing you use, but you should use the same method for your whole piece of work.

Figure 5.15 shows the details that you should include if you are referencing an article on a website: author, date of publication, title of the article and website address. For all online material you must include the date you looked at it. Websites can change and your reference should allow a reader to find the source themselves, if they want to read more on the topic. If you use books or magazines, you should provide the author's name, the name of the publication, name of publisher and date of publication. You can provide your references in a list at the end of your report, called a **bibliography**.

1. Logan, S., Irvine, S. (2020) *Practising Changes for the Future*. London: Tudor Rose Press.
2. Rosane O. (2022) *Ethiopia's Banana-Like Enset Is Potentially a Climate Superfood That Can Reduce Global Hunger* [Online] www.treehugger.com (Accessed 4 Feb 2022)
3. Bull, J. (2022) 'Climate change and pollution solutions'. *News of the Day*, 3 August 2022, p. 8.

Figure 5.15: Example of a book, a website and newspaper article in a bibliography

KEY TERM

citing: quoting from or mentioning a particular author or a publication when you use their material, in the main body of the work.

KEY TERM

bibliography: a list of sources referred to in a report or essay printed at the end of the written work.

TIP

For Cambridge IGCSE and O Level Global Perspectives, there is no fixed method of citation and referencing; you can use any one method that suits you. But you should use only one method, to make your citation and referencing clear.

Alternatively, you can put the references in footnotes: these are small notes giving details of sources at the bottom of each page.

Every citation in your essay should link to a reference, whether the reference is in a footnote or a bibliography. The easiest way to do this is to number your sources in a reference list at the end of your report and put the relevant number wherever you use material from that source.

So if the example reference in Figure 5.15 was numbered 1 in the list, you would type [1] (in superscript) wherever you used information or quoted from that article.

ACTIVITY 5.17

1 Read the extract below, which relates to the topic Education for all, and locate the citations, quotes or references. When you have found them, write them in the table below.

The United Nations Convention on the Rights of the Child from 1990 recognises education as a legal right of every child (UNICEF, 1990). Yet education remains a privilege to many. UNESCO data shows that '258 million children and youth were out of school' (UNESCO, 2019) for the school year ending in 2018. Of that total, more than 129 million were girls and 58 million were of primary school age. Among those fortunate to have access to education, on the other hand, more than '617 million children and adolescents' (UNESCO, 2017) do not have minimum proficiency levels in reading and mathematics.

Education is the process where an individual acquires or imparts basic knowledge to another. It is also where a person:

- develops skills essential to daily living
- learns social norms
- develops judgement and reasoning
- learns how to discern right from wrong.

The ultimate goal of education is to help an individual navigate life and contribute to society once they become older.

There are various types of education, but typically traditional schooling dictates the way a person's education success is measured. People who attended school and attained a higher level of education are considered more employable and are likely to earn more.

In developing, low-income countries, for example, the Centre for Global Development (2005) estimates there is a projected 10 per cent increase in a person's future income for every additional year of education.

Source: Abridged from: www.worldvision.ca

Education helps eradicate poverty and hunger (UNESCO, 2010), giving people the chance at better lives. This is one of the biggest reasons why parents strive to make their kids attend school for as long as possible. It is also why nations work towards promoting easier access to education for both children and adults.

There are plenty of reasons why education is important. Generally speaking, they all tie closely to a person's goals in life and to their future well-being. Below are some of the other most common reasons education is so important:

- Education helps a person hone their communication skills by learning how to read, write, speak and listen.
- Education develops critical thinking. This is vital in teaching a person how to use logic when making decisions and interacting with people (for example, boosting creativity, enhancing time management).
- Education helps an individual meet basic job qualifications and makes them more likely to secure better jobs.
- Education promotes gender equality and helps empower girls and women. A World Bank report (1994) found that an extra year of schooling for girls reduced teen pregnancy rates by 6 per cent and gave women more control over how many children they have.
- Education reduces child mortality. Studies have shown that a child born to a mother who can read is 50 per cent more likely to survive past the age of five.

CONTINUED

	Claim, reference to another source, or quote from the text	Citation or reference
1	United Nations Convention on the Rights of the Child	UNICEF, 1990
2		
3		
4		
5		
6		

2   Compare your table with a partner's.

  • Did either of you miss anything, or did you have the same ideas?

  • Do you feel confident about citing and referencing in your individual report?

SHOWCASING YOUR SKILLS

Research

Now you have the chance to use your skills to research and write a short report.

1   Select a topic and decide on an important issue. (Your teacher may help you with this.)

2   Look online for any opinions about the issue.

3   Choose two different opinions. Make a note of the perspectives. Are they global, national or local?

4   Select your sources and, for each source, if it is from the internet note the web address, author (if there is an author), the date you looked at the website, and the date of the article (if the article is dated). Copy and paste the web address into your record and note the title of the article. For print-based sources you will need to record the author's name, the title of the publication, the name of the publisher and the date of publication. If you only read a chapter from a whole book you should also record the pages you looked at.

5   Make a note of what the two perspectives are, any evidence the sources provide and the reasons why they think what they do.

6   If you feel you have enough information about your topic/issue, plan your short report:

  • Start with a title or a question for your report (your teacher might help you with this). The easiest way to do this is to have a question to which one of your sources would answer no and the other would answer yes.

CONTINUED

- In your plan you should include an introduction (explaining the issue and why it is a problem).

- Provide some information about the issue using relevant evidence. Don't forget to cite any quotes that you have used.

- Identify the two perspectives.

- Explain each perspective separately in your own words.

- Include a conclusion. (What your perspective is. Have you changed your mind after reading about the issue and the two different perspectives?) Answer your question.

7   Write your report in essay form, using your plan.

8   At the end of the essay, list your sources. For online sources list the information about the author, the date, the web address, the name of the article and the date you accessed the website. For print sources list the author, the date of publication, the title of the publication, the publisher name and publisher location.

The essay should be about 500 words – not including references.

Research reminders

Focus your research by choosing search terms that will lead to relevant sources of information and perspectives.

Make sure you keep a note of which sources might be helpful to you.

Keep a note of websites you visit, information about any sources you might use, information about the author and the article so that you can cite them in your work and provide references for all sources.

Reflection on your showcase

Write a few lines describing what went well in your short research report.

Did you manage to find two different perspectives?

Did you keep a note of your sources?

Did you write a plan? Was the plan helpful?

What have you learned about research?

Are you happy with your essay? What would you do differently another time?

SUMMARY

In this chapter you have been exploring research skills. You have looked at how you might choose a topic/issue to research and you have been thinking about and practising planning research and selecting appropriate sources.

You have looked at some examples of evidence for selection to support perspectives. You have considered how to find relevant information and how primary research can be used effectively.

You have thought about how to make notes and practised paraphrasing source material for use in your work. You have considered the importance of organising your research, and have practised keeping a record of research and sources, understanding why that is important. You have thought about the ways you can avoid plagiarism.

You have used all these skills to work on a short report.

REVIEW AND REFLECTION

	I have learned about …	I need more practice with …
Choosing a topic and issue to research		
Planning my research		
Finding and selecting relevant information		
Conducting research, including selecting the most appropriate research methods		
Keeping a record of my research and recording my findings		
Writing up a research report		
Why avoiding plagiarism is important and how to cite and reference the sources I have used		

> Chapter 6
Communication

This chapter will concentrate on building productive communication skills, including skills in reading and listening, speaking and writing. You will learn some strategies for reading and listening to different types of texts, as well as strategies to improve fluency in your speech and writing. You will learn how to present effectively to an audience and will develop your debating skills by looking at an issue from both sides. You will learn how to plan and present arguments clearly, using connectives to help your audience follow your explanations. You will also develop ways to structure your writing, and practise writing an introduction and a conclusion to an essay.

Topics that are explored in this chapter include: Climate change, energy and resources (sustainable living), Migration and urbanisation, Transport, travel and tourism (mass tourism), Technology, industry and innovation (technology in healthcare), and Education for all.

BEFORE YOU START

Communication skills are needed for everything we do. Even when we do a self-reflection activity we are using language to think about ourselves and writing to communicate these thoughts.

Look at the following communication skills:

speaking in public   debating   essay writing   listening to others

writing my own opinion   reading for details   skim reading

Which of these skills do you think is your strongest? Which do you think you need to develop most? Rate your ability with each skill from 1–10, with 10 being your area of strength and 1 being your area for development as you begin this chapter.

6.1 Reading

The Cambridge IGCSE and O Level Global Perspectives course involves reading from a variety of different sources to identify issues, perspectives and evidence and to draw conclusions. As well as reading narrative text you will come across other types of information such as poems, presentations, diagrams, cartoon strips, graphs and statistics that you will need to read and understand before you use them. You will need to use different reading strategies to understand and respond to texts. This section focuses on the strategies needed to be able to understand written texts.

REFLECTION

Why do you think it is important for you to be able to read and understand different types of text while following the Cambridge IGCSE and O Level Global Perspectives course? What strategies do you think might help you do this?

Reading strategies

Strategies you can use before, during and after reading a text are shown in the following table.

Before reading	During reading	After reading
Predict from the title what the text might be about.	Highlight ten key words to enable someone else to identify what the text is about.	Give your opinion about the text, giving reasons for your opinion.
Identify five words you expect to find in the text.	Summarise the first paragraph in one sentence.	Sum up the text in one paragraph.
Create possible sentences that might appear in the text from given word pairs.	Identify specific details, e.g. perspectives, issues, evidence.	Use the RAFT writing strategy – questions to enable you to understand texts by examining role, audience, format and topic.

The RAFT writing strategy focuses on the following:

Role of the writer: Who is the writer? A professor? A journalist? An employee? A politician?

Audience: For whom is the writing intended? The government? A fan club? Fellow students?

Format: In what format is the writing? A personal letter? A report? A news article? A blog post?

Topic: What is the writing about? Which perspectives can be seen? Is anything missing or not properly explained? Is the evidence credible?

ACTIVITY 6.01

1 Practise the following strategies before you read the text that follows:

a Predict what you think a text with the following title might be about:

'Does globalisation bring about more harm than good?'

CONTINUED

b   See if you can write some sentences from the following word pairs to identify some of the content of the text of globalisation. For example, for the first pair you might have: 'Globalisation has failed to reduce poverty around the world.'

failed	poverty
force	development
riches	everyone
gap	widening
globalisation	worked

2   Read the following section of text about globalisation and check your sentences against it.

> It is clear that globalisation has failed to rid the world of poverty. Rather than being an unstoppable force for development, globalisation now seems more like an economic temptress, promising riches to everyone but only delivering to the few. Although global average per capita income rose strongly throughout the 20th century, the income gap between rich and poor countries has been widening for many decades. Globalisation has not worked.
>
> *Source: www.theguardian.com*

The words shown in the word pairs are the key words you might have highlighted in the text when reading.

3   Summarise this paragraph in one sentence.

Figure 6.1: Reading strategies help you select the information you need

DISCUSSION

Compare your sentences and summaries with a partner. Did you capture the same points? To summarise the sentence, you could have written: 'Globalisation has not worked because poverty still exists and the gap between rich and poor is getting wider.'

How to skim read

Skim reading, or reading for **gist**, means you do not read the whole text word for word. You can use titles, sub-titles, key words, pictures and captions to help you understand the content of the text. Reading the first sentence and last sentence can also be useful when skim reading. You will use skim reading as a strategy when you are researching. Skim reading will help you quickly evaluate what you are reading and decide if it is useful to your research and whether you should go back and read it in detail.

KEY TERM

gist: the general meaning of a piece of text.

ACTIVITY 6.02

Imagine you have decided that you would like to do an essay on the topic of Migration and urbanisation. You are especially interested in how family life is affected by migration for economic reasons. You have found the following article and need to consider whether it is useful for your work or not. Remember, numerical statistics can change over time, don't forget to cross check with the most recent sources.

1 Skim read the article and decide if the article is useful for your essay. Share your reasons with a partner.

> ### Migration crisis: 'Who can refuse these human beings? Who?' asks UN official
>
> The Mediterranean migration crisis is a 'human atrocity' on a scale not seen since the second world war and can be tackled only with short-term generosity from European nations and a sustained global push to reduce extreme poverty over the coming decades, a senior United Nations official has warned.
>
> Philippe Douste-Blazy, a UN undersecretary-general and former French foreign minister, said the world had to understand that economic inequality was driving people from their home countries just as steadily as war.
>
> Douste-Blazy – who advises the UN secretary general on innovative financing for development and chairs Unitaid, which uses small levies on air fares to fund health programmes – also said migration to richer countries would increase unless more was done to improve life in the developing world.
>
> 'The wave was 10cm high two years ago,' he said. 'Now it's about 40cm high. But for your children, it will be 30 metres high. Why? Because 2 billion people in the world earn less than $1.25 a day. The difference between now and 20 years ago is that everybody looks at everybody now – it's the globalisation of the economy and the globalisation of communications: internet, TV, radio. It's very new.'
>
> While he acknowledged that many refugees were fleeing violence and oppression in countries such as Syria, Eritrea, Somalia and Sudan, Douste-Blazy said 'we have 50% who are trying to escape from extreme poverty'.
>
> *Source: www.theguardian.com*

CONTINUED

2   Now skim read the following text:

Does migration change life for the better for people from poor countries?

The report collated data collected by Gallup about the experiences of 25 000 migrants and 441 000 non-migrants in 150 countries. Respondents were asked what they have gained and lost through migration, how satisfied they are with their lives, whether they find it more difficult to find jobs or start a business, and whether they are likelier to report health problems.

The findings suggested the greatest gains in wellbeing come from migration to rich countries. Migrants moving from one rich country to another – the UK to Canada, for instance – reported the highest levels of life satisfaction, financial security, personal safety, and health.

In contrast, migrants who moved between developing countries – Indonesia to Malaysia, for example – seemed to fare similarly or worse, according to the report. They were also identified as the group least likely to feel optimistic about their lives.

According to Gallup data only 8% of adult migrants in developing countries, and 27% in rich countries, reported sending 'financial help' to family in another country.

Source: www.theguardian.com

Decide which article is more suitable for your purpose. Would you use both? If so, why? Note down the parts of the article(s) that you think would be useful, and write one sentence explaining how you would use it.

Figure 6.2: Migration to other countries happens for a variety of reasons

How to scan

Scanning involves looking for specific information in the text you are reading such as a date, a specific fact or an opinion. Like skimming, you do not have to read every word. It is a good idea to write down specific questions that you want answers to, so that you know what you are scanning for.

ACTIVITY 6.03

Scan the text in Activity 6.02 part 2 to find the following information. Underline where the information is in the text.

1   How many countries did Gallup collect data from?

2   What percentage of adult migrants send financial help home to their families in developing countries?

6.2 Listening

Listening skills are important for activities done in class and when working with others. Good listening shows that you understand, that you are interested in what others say and that you have empathy. People will feel that their ideas are worthwhile if you listen to them. This will increase their confidence and you will get different perspectives about issues and information that you may not previously have considered. Texts that you listen to such as films, podcasts, advertisements, speeches, songs and documentaries can provide useful information and ideas that you could use when you are researching.

ACTIVITY 6.04

Are you an **effective**, **active** listener?

1   Complete the quiz below to see how good an effective and active listener you are. Try to be as honest as you can.

	Statement	Yes	No
1	I listen more than I talk.		
2	I maintain good eye contact.		
3	I try not to give too much advice.		
4	I look interested when someone else is speaking.		
5	I wait for someone to finish before I start speaking.		
6	I give positive comments as feedback.		
7	I use appropriate body language (nod, shake head).		
8	I ask questions that show I'm listening.		

TIPS

The type of reading strategy you use will depend on the reason you are reading. These reasons include:

*   for gist (skim reading)

*   for specific detail (scanning)

*   to acquire new vocabulary

*   for developing ideas and adding evidence

*   out of interest.

KEY TERMS

active listening: the process in which the listener takes active responsibility to understand the content and feeling of what is being said and then checks with the speaker to see if they heard what the speaker intended to communicate.

effective listening: listening to the words of the speaker and the meaning of the words.

CONTINUED

	Statement	Yes	No
9	I avoid other distractions like looking at my phone or texting while listening.		
10	I don't assume I know what the other person is talking about.		

The more you answered 'yes', the more developed your listening skills are.

2   For any statement that you answered 'no' to, consider its importance and how you are going to develop your listening skills further.

ACTIVITY 6.05

1   Pair up with a partner. Let them talk for one minute about what global issues are important to them and why. You should encourage your partner to share their opinions and justifications for these opinions by listening actively.

After one minute it is your turn to ask your partner questions about what they have said. You should ask about things they said that you found interesting and find out more about their reasoning for their personal opinions.

2   Swap roles and repeat the activity.

3   Evaluate your listening skills by writing a quick reflection on the following questions:

a   How did you feel in each role?

b   Do you feel that you learned something from listening to your partner completing this activity? What was it?

c   Did you get distracted?

d   How could you improve your listening skills?

4   Now evaluate your partner's listening skills using the following questions:

a   Did you feel your partner listened to you actively and effectively?

b   Was there anything you noticed during the activity that made you feel your partner was or wasn't listening to you?

c   How do you think your partner could improve their listening skills?

5   Share your feedback with your partner.

Listening strategies

Strategies you can use before, during and after listening to a text are shown in the following table:

Before listening	During listening	After listening
Predict from the title of the text what the text might be about and how many people might be speaking.	Use visuals and make notes to recall what the text is about.	Write down the main issue and at least two supporting details.
Write down six words or phrases that you expect to hear.	Write questions prompted by what you are listening to.	Reproduce the message of the text orally.
Identify what you want to know before listening and produce a table to collect information as you hear it (who, what, when, where, why, how, cause, effect, impact, etc.).	Write down specific details for further research, e.g. perspectives, issues, evidence.	Give your opinion about the text, giving reasons for your opinion.

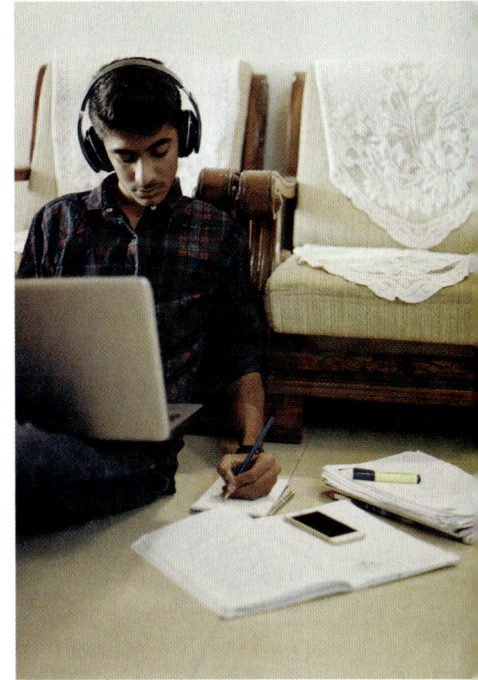

Figure 6.3: Using before, during and after strategies helps you to listen more effectively

ACTIVITY 6.06

1 Use your search engine to find a short video clip using the search term 'Education for all'. Predict what you think the clip will be about and six words you might hear during the clip.

2 Watch and listen to the video clip.

3 After listening, write down what the main issue was and at least two supporting details.

4 Write down any other things you heard that you found interesting from the video clip.

5 What was your opinion of the video clip? Give at least one reason for your opinion.

6 Can you identify any areas that need further research or explanation? Write them down as questions.

DISCUSSION

How did you find your listening skills in Activity 6.06? Discuss your thoughts in a small group.

You will probably have identified what the clip was about from visuals and words used in the opening part of the video. You might also have noticed the change in **tone** of the clip (music and presenter's voice) once it moved from the issue to the courses of action towards the end (the tone becoming more optimistic and upbeat). The pictures and statistics given will have helped you identify supporting details for the main issue.

KEY TERM

tone: a quality in the voice of the speaker that expresses the speaker's feelings or thoughts, often towards the person being spoken to or the topic being spoken about. It can also refer to expressions of mood in music.

6.3 Speaking

Speaking is a skill that many of us take for granted. Effective speaking involves being able to speak in a public context clearly and with confidence, but at the same time showing your own personality. Skills in speaking clearly, confidently and in a reasoned way can be developed, like the other communication skills examined in this chapter.

Speaking in public can be difficult and awkward for many people. When you are at home or with friends, you can generally speak in the way that you want to. However, when speaking in class and in public, there are certain **conventions** to follow. The key to really getting confident at public speaking is practice. You can practise by carrying out pair and small group discussions and by reading aloud or speaking aloud when you are alone.

KEY TERM

convention: a custom or a way of acting or doing something that is widely accepted and followed.

Figure 6.4: Speaking with confidence takes practice

Reading aloud

It is important to get used to the sound of your own voice. The best way to get used to how you sound when speaking is to make a recording. You can do this at home – perhaps using a mobile phone or a computer. You can record yourself and listen back to see where you have rushed or not been clear.

ACTIVITY 6.07

1   Find a short article to read aloud, for example the following one about sustainable living.

Why we promote sustainable living

Our planet can only produce a finite number of resources – from food, to water – and can only withstand a certain degree of greenhouse gas emissions in order to stay healthy. We only have one Earth and are utterly dependent on it for our survival and well-being. But both people and nature are facing severe consequences if our current consumption increases (that's the amount of energy we use and our demand for resources to feed, clothe and house us, as well as materials that we want for pure enjoyment).

The biggest driver of environmental degradation is the fact that we're consuming resources at an unsustainable rate, and therefore our production of goods is increasing. This is often a result of economic growth – from affluent Westerners to growing wealth in the developing world.

Much of the planet's economic growth has been achieved as a result of over-exploiting resources, such as fossil fuels. But as the world's resources are coming under increasing pressure, so the constraints to growth are becoming increasingly visible.

Source: www.wwf.org.uk

2   Read the article through silently to yourself first.

3   Read the article aloud in your normal speaking voice. Don't worry if you make mistakes, just continue to read to the end.

4   Read the article again, and this time record yourself as you are reading. You will use this recording to compare with another recording in the next activity.

Chunking text to aid fluency

A strategy you can use to help when you are reading out loud is called **chunking**. When you have a large amount of information to read, breaking it into smaller chunks helps you to control the speed at which you speak and add interest to what you are saying. We can chunk what we read into smaller pieces by using marks to show us where the breaks are. Generally, about five or six words should be in each chunk; however, sometimes longer or shorter chunks are used when emphasising an important point.

KEY TERM

chunking: breaking down information into smaller, more manageable pieces.

ACTIVITY 6.08

1 Try reading this short article aloud again, paying attention to where the chunks are.

Why we promote sustainable living

Our planet can only produce a finite number of resources – from food, to water – and can only withstand | a certain degree of greenhouse gas emissions in order to stay healthy. | We only have one Earth | and are utterly dependent on it for our survival and well-being. | But | both people and nature are facing severe consequences if our current consumption increases | (that's the amount of energy we use| and our demand for resources to feed, | clothe | and house us, | as well as materials that we want for pure enjoyment). |

The biggest driver of environmental degradation | is the fact that we're consuming resources at an unsustainable rate, | and therefore our production of goods is increasing. | This is often a result of economic growth – | from affluent Westerners | to growing wealth in the developing world.

Much of the planet's economic growth has been achieved as a result of over-exploiting resources, | such as fossil fuels. | But as the world's resources are coming under increasing pressure, | so the constraints to growth are becoming increasingly visible.

Source: www.wwf.org.uk

2 Read the article through silently to yourself first.

3 Read the article aloud using the chunks in your normal speaking voice.

4 Read the article aloud again, this time recording yourself as you are reading. Compare this recording with your first recording. Which one is better? What makes it more effective? Write down what you noticed about the difference between the recordings and which one you preferred.

Other tips for reading aloud

When reading aloud, try to remember the following:

- Don't rush. You may feel you want to speed up and get it over with quickly, but this will cause you to mumble, making it difficult for people to understand what you are trying to say.

- Use varied intonation. Using the same tone of voice can give the impression that the speaker is bored.

- Try to hold the text at eye level, rather than lowering your head to read it, and project your voice as if you were talking to someone at the back of the room.

- Try to pause for a couple of seconds at the end of a sentence or paragraph. Pausing also allows you to emphasise key points and gives your audience time to take in what you have said.

Presenting effectively to an audience

When you are presenting your ideas to an audience, you can do this in many ways, for example via a computer, a role-play, a recorded video, a talk, or a formal presentation. In every case you should think of who the audience is and how you could present your ideas to engage your audience with what you are saying. Speaking effectively means that you will need to practise what you are going to say and how you are going to say it before you present it to your audience. The more often you practise, the more prepared you will be and the more confident you will feel.

Presenting well also includes:

- How you use your notes – they should be referred to when you need them but not read.

- Looking at your audience or the computer camera.

- Speaking clearly, using pauses and not rushing.

- Being ready to deal with interruptions or questions.

- Trying to engage your audience with what you are saying.

ACTIVITY 6.09

1   Look at worldslargestlesson.globalgoals.org from UNICEF and click the 'Themes and Collections' tab. Then find the 'Sharing stories from changemakers' link and watch how some young people are sharing their stories and presenting their ideas.

As you watch their presentations tick yes or no in the table below:

Presentation skill	Yes	No
Does the presenter look confident?		
Are they standing still and making eye contact with the camera?		
Do they speak well – not speaking too fast or too slowly?		
Are they reading from notes or a script?		
Do they use appropriate gestures?		
Do they engage you as part of their audience?		

2   After watching the clip(s) write a reflection about what things you could improve when you speak to an audience. You might also reflect on what they say as well as how they say it.

There are many benefits of presenting well that will extend beyond your time at school. You will need to be able to speak effectively and present yourself well at job interviews, college interviews, or just meeting people for the first time. Many workplaces use presentations as a common way of getting a message across; you will have also noticed that presentations are given by your teachers and your school leaders regularly.

When creating presentations, keep the following in mind:

- Who is the intended audience (younger children, teenagers, parents, etc.)?

- What is the purpose of the presentation (persuasion, informative, advice, etc.)? How does the purpose affect the language (if it is to persuade then persuasive language should be used) and tone you should use?

- Is it a suitable length? It must not be too long – remember the attention span of most people is quite short (psychologists suggest about three minutes!). Therefore break the presentation down into different sections of about three minutes with something to stimulate the audience between each one – perhaps some humour or an interesting graphic or a cartoon to reinforce a point.

- How are you making it engaging? An effective presentation needs to be engaging and 'grab the attention' of the intended audience, especially if you are trying to get something from the audience and/or persuade them to do something. Consider asking a quick question, giving some options for the answer and getting the audience to vote on what they think the answer is.

- What illustrations and examples are you using and why are you using them? It is important to use illustrations to help people understand key points and perspectives, especially if you want them to take action.

- How will you perform your presentation? Tables or lecterns can be very useful for formal presentations but can make it difficult to connect with your audience. Use notes rather than a script and avoid reading straight from your notes.

ACTIVITY 6.10

1   Look at Figure 6.5 which shows the slide from a presentation aimed at raising awareness about litter and the need to keep the environment clean so that disease does not spread.

What can we do
- Start a petition
- Volunteer to clean up
- Stop throwing litter
- Recycle

Figure 6.5: Giving a presentation

2   Answer the following questions:

a   What are the strengths of this presentation slide? (Give at least two.)

b   What needs improving?

3   Discuss your evaluation of the presentation slide with a partner to share your ideas.

4   On your own or with your partner, design a slide that you think would work better. You might like to find a copyright-free photograph online if you would prefer to use a different image.

5   Look at other pairs' slides and make a note of things they changed.

ACTIVITY 6.11

In this activity, you will prepare a short presentation to practise your presentation skills.

1   Choose a picture that relates to one of the global topics. Figure 6.6 shows one you could use that falls within the topic of Migration and urbanisation.

Figure 6.6: You could use this image as a prompt for the activity

2   Create a short presentation (no more than two minutes long) about the picture. Make notes but not a script. Notes should take the form of bullet points to act as prompts.

3   Be prepared to answer questions about the picture and the wider topic for a further two minutes.

4   In pairs, share your presentation for two minutes without interruption.

5   Ask your partner questions about their picture and about the wider topic for two minutes (not repeating what you have already heard).

6   Swap over and repeat the activity with another picture that your partner has chosen.

TIPS

- Speaking skills need practice like any other skill.

- Public speaking needs as much practice and preparation as report writing.

- Presentations should be created and given for a purpose, not be too long, and be informative and engaging.

REFLECTION

Did you find the exercise in Activity 6.11 a good way of developing your speaking skills? How might you use what you have learned from this exercise in the future? Write down two things that you are already doing when you speak and two things that you need to improve on.

6.4 Presenting an argument

To argue successfully when speaking or writing involves balancing different viewpoints and evidence that supports and challenges your viewpoint. Arguments, discussions and **debates** are part of our daily lives. They help us to express our own opinions and perspectives, but also help us to use empathy when listening to others' perspectives. A strong argument can make you review your own opinion and perhaps persuade you to change your **standpoint**, or it may strengthen your opinion further.

To create and communicate an effective argument your knowledge of your topic needs to be strong. You will need to make sure you have completed thorough research before you start. Research on a topic will help you understand the perspectives that are held and the arguments they use to prove their point. You can use these ideas to build 'for' and 'against' points for your own argument. You will need to be confident in your knowledge, including the examples and evidence you are going to present. Most importantly arguments need to be balanced – this involves considering claims both for and against an argument. This shows you have considered both sides of the argument, which will make your own thoughts and conclusions on the topic more compelling.

KEY TERMS

debate: a formal discussion on a particular issue in a public meeting, in which opposing arguments are put forward and which usually ends in a vote.

standpoint: a point of view, attitude, position, way of thinking or perspective.

Figure 6.7: Successful arguments present claims for and against in a balanced way

Claims for — Claims against

TIP

To construct a strong argument, you will require skills in analysis, evaluation and research. Chapters 3, 4 and 5 of this book help you to develop these skills.

ACTIVITY 6.12

In this activity you will prepare 'for' and 'against' arguments.

Figure 6.8: Is climate change the biggest issue in human history?

CONTINUED

1 Look at Figure 6.8 and make notes about the following:

- What are your own thoughts on the topic?

- Ask five people in your class what their thoughts are on this topic. Do their views align with yours or do they provide an alternative view?

- Can you balance both sides of the argument? If not, you will need to think about arguments you could make to balance the two sides.

2 Create a table with two columns, one with 'For' as the heading and one with 'Against' as the heading. List the strongest points from your notes to answer the question 'Is climate change the biggest issue in human history?' You will need to balance the amount of points on both sides so they are equal.

3 Weighing up both sides of the argument, write a paragraph summarising the 'for' and 'against' points made and conclude with your own opinion on which argument you think is stronger. Has your opinion changed from your original thoughts you noted down?

If you are taking part in a debate, a more one-sided, persuasive argument is needed in response to the proposal for debate. This also involves balancing the argument by anticipating the counter arguments of your opponent and refuting any challenges they may come up with. A conclusion to a debate will end with a strong reason why the audience should agree with your standpoint (the point of view that you are presenting). Debates will often have a chairperson who will announce the proposal, call on the debaters to deliver their speeches (the order of speakers will be agreed before the debate begins), and keep time on the speakers to make sure both sides are balanced.

ACTIVITY 6.13

In this activity you will practise presenting an argument 'for' or 'against' a proposal.

Imagine that you are taking part in a debate. The proposal is:

'Technology is destroying family life.'

1 Choose someone to pair with to debate one of the following three proposals:

- Animal testing should be banned.

- Renewable forms of energy should be subsidised by the government.

- All students should be allowed to use mobile phones and other electronic devices during lessons.

2 With your partner, decide which one of you is going to argue 'for' the proposal and which will argue 'against' it.

TIP

When you are shaping your argument for a presentation or debate, you may find it helpful to use connectives such as 'to begin with', 'similarly', 'alternatively, 'moreover', 'as a consequence' or 'for example'. You will find further ideas for connectives in the next section.

CONTINUED

3 Prepare a persuasive argument in support of your standpoint. You may need to do some further research to gain ideas and evidence to use in your argument, but you should always use your own words in the debate. Don't forget to anticipate what counter arguments or challenges your partner may come up with.

4 Ask a third member of your class to act as the chairperson for the debate.

5 Once the debate is over, agree on who had the most convincing argument (the chairperson gets the final say).

6.5 Writing

You write to communicate with others. To communicate clearly, you will have to structure your writing so that it is easy to follow, with your ideas in a logical order. Your arguments, evidence and perspectives should be presented clearly and in a cohesive way. If your writing is too short or is not structured, that makes it difficult for your reader to understand fully or follow what you are trying to communicate. You will also have to practise writing sentences with varied lengths and show that you can control punctuation. For extended written tasks, you will need to spend time revising what you have written and edit your work to improve how it reads.

Planning a piece of written work

When writing a report or essay, or tackling a similar piece of written work, it is always a good idea to plan out your report or essay early on, so that you have a clear idea of what you need to find out and then what you will write. This helps you to remember everything you need to include.

A typical essay will include the following:

- Introduction
- The main body of the essay (where you set out your arguments)
- Conclusion
- Reference list (where you list the sources you have used).

You will be able to convey your ideas clearly if you use a structured series of **paragraphs** to present your arguments. Text is divided into paragraphs to make it easier to follow and to separate new ideas or themes. Paragraphs go further than just an explanatory sentence, and many paragraphs make up the body of an extended piece of writing like an essay or a report. A paragraph could be four or five sentences long, but is not usually longer than half a page. Each paragraph should convey a main idea (the **topic sentence**), followed by **supporting sentences** and evidence.

KEY TERMS

cohesive: fitting together well, each part following logically, so that a reader can read through and follow the whole argument. Each paragraph should be cohesive, and each paragraph should follow on logically from the last one, making the whole essay cohesive.

paragraph: a section of writing containing one main idea or part of an argument, presented in a clear and logical way.

topic sentence: the sentence that expresses the main idea in a paragraph; usually the first sentence in the paragraph.

supporting sentence: a sentence that gives information, an explanation and/or examples to support the topic sentence.

If you have made summaries of your notes and thoughts when doing your research, you may find that you can use these to build a paragraph plan for the main body of your essay. Writing a paragraph plan can help to clarify your thoughts when you start and will make it easier to check, change or improve parts of your essay, or to move paragraphs to make your essay more logical and readable. You write down the topic sentences of your paragraphs and decide if it follows a cohesive structure (refer to the blank table below to see how you might structure this).

Paragraph	Content

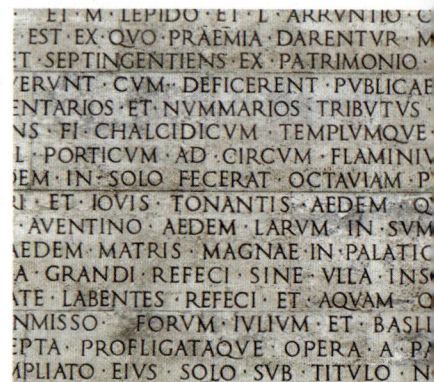

Figure 6.9: Use paragraphs to make your writing easier to follow

Table 6.1 gives guidance on planning a report or essay that aims to research a global issue and recommend a course of action to help address it. It will help you determine what you should include in your writing and give you a possible way to decide what you need to do and find out about, and then write about your issue.

Table 6.1: Example planning guideline for a research report on a global issue

Section	Planning guidance
Topic/Issue	Select a topic from the list of Cambridge IGCSE and O Level Global Perspectives topics and one issue/problem related to that topic. You will only research and write about the issue you have selected.
Research question	Write a clear, global question about your chosen issue. The question should allow you to include different perspectives (global, national and local) on the issue you have selected.
Introduction	Give a brief explanation of the question and the issue and some details that show the reader that this is a global issue. You can also introduce the perspectives – this will lead into the next section.
Analysis	Analyse the issue from different perspectives (two sources for each perspective) providing information to support these perspectives. Explain the different causes and consequences of the issue. Analyse different possible courses of action related to different causes/consequences.

Section	Planning guidance
Evaluation	Evaluate the courses of action and your preferred course of action. Explain why that is the best/most effective course of action. Evaluate the evidence and the sources you found and used to support the arguments.
Reflection	Write an outline of your own perspective and what you have learned about the issue. Explain how your perspective has been changed by your research, the evidence presented and others' perspectives. Write a detailed and supported answer to the question.
Reference list	Provide a list of sources used within the report.

ACTIVITY 6.14

1   Read the questions below. Choose one as the research question for a report and complete steps **2–7** to help you in your essay planning:

- Does the internet have a positive role to play in the lives of young people?

- Should female and male sportspeople be paid the same?

- Do the dangers of artificial intelligence outweigh the benefits?

- Do we need a free press?

- Is education the solution to the global water crisis?

- Is globalisation beneficial for developing countries?

- Is fake news damaging to society?

- Should we stop air travel for leisure?

- Is tourism damaging to local culture?

- Can art change society?

- Whose responsibility is it to stop water pollution?

- Is job creation the answer to poverty?

- Does social media cause political polarisation?

- Can trade support sustainable development?

TIPS

- To achieve the best outcome, you need to plan all the work you do. Plans should be SMART.

- Plan your report before you start work so that your teacher can guide you if appropriate.

- The better you plan your essay or report, the easier you will find it to write it.

CONTINUED

2   Make sure you are clear as to what issue is under discussion:

　　a   What is the issue?

　　b   Why is it an issue?

　　c   Could it be a global issue?

3   Draw up a plan for an individual research report on the question you chose. Your plan should fit onto one A4 sheet of paper and follow the planning guidance from Table 6.1.

4   Can you identify two different arguments to the question? Could these be used as different perspectives?

5   Make a note of what research you will need to do so that you have information about:

　　•   the issue, including the global scale and in your own country

　　•   causes and consequences

　　•   at least two different perspectives including one global and one national

　　•   possible courses of action.

6   What is your personal view about this issue?

7   Share your plan with your group. Discuss each other's plans and give each other feedback. How is your plan different from other plans? Are there similarities? Make notes of any good ideas and feedback that have been given to you.

Note: In this activity you will not go so far as to evaluate the possible courses of action or provide a reference list. However, you will need to perform these steps for any report or essay that you submit to your teacher.

DISCUSSION

Why is planning so important for an individual research report?

Do you think it is helpful to start with a question before you begin researching?

Writing a report or essay

In Chapter 5 you practised strategies for writing a research essay or report such as taking notes and writing summaries of your research findings. Once you have assembled your notes and summaries and written your essay plan, you are ready to begin work on your first draft.

You don't need to write a report or essay in one session. You can even start in the middle. Rather than staring at a blank page, skip the introduction and jump in at paragraph two. You can come back and write the introductory paragraph at the top when you have finished.

Figure 6.10: It can be difficult to get started with writing – don't hide from it

Writing an introduction to an essay on a global issue

The most common structure for an essay is an introduction, the essay body and then a conclusion. The introduction is the part of the essay where you explain to the reader what your essay will be about, maybe give an explanation of your research question, and give them a hint about what you will be exploring and why it is important.

When you write an essay or report about a global issue, you should explain clearly what the issue is and why it is a global issue and outline your question and what the different perspectives are that you will be telling the reader about.

You can write the introduction first, presenting your view on your question, but for longer essays, some people actually write it later, once they have a clear idea of what they are going to write about. It is up to you what you decide. However, it is helpful to write a first draft of your introduction early on, so that you have a clear idea of what you are going to focus on and what you are not going to include.

Here are some suggestions to help you make sure you have included everything to help your reader understand what your essay or report is going to be about:

- Start your essay with the introduction: one or at most two paragraphs.

- The introduction will explain the issue you will be addressing.

- It will tell the reader why this is an important issue and show that it is a global issue.

- It will provide the reader with what you thought about the issue before you researched it. If you have found that different people have different perspectives about it, outline those in a few words. (Depending on your question you might outline different possible answers to the question.)

- Make sure that when someone has read your introduction, they are clear about what you are going to write about.

ACTIVITY 6.15

1   Read this introduction to an individual research report.

The title of the report is:

> 'Will modern technology have a good effect on healthcare for all the world?'

Read the introduction through once and then check against the suggestions above to see if it is doing all the things an introduction should do. Then look at the questions that follow.

> In the past, healthcare was analogue. We did not use machinery or technology for health, the machines and technology did not exist. These days we have modern medical treatment that works well and makes our lives better and helps medical staff to work more easily. They can keep accurate records, and easily check on patients' medical history. They can prescribe the right drugs for the right people. Even though technology is very helpful in healthcare these days, it can also be very risky. Medical systems can be hacked, and mistakes can be made when people depend on technology instead of their own observations. I am not sure whether technology is really beneficial for all humanity or whether it could be a danger. I think maybe if doctors and healthcare workers are trained only using technology, then people in developing countries will suffer. This is because I believe many healthcare workers train in developed countries and then return home as professionals. I am going to research different perspectives about this question, and I will try to decide if modern technology will be good for everyone, or not.

a   Is it clear why technology in healthcare might be an important issue?

b   Is it clear that it could be a global issue?

c   Is it clear that there are at least two possible perspectives on this issue? What are they?

d   Do we know what the writer's perspective is?

e   Do we know what the writer is going to try to find out?

f   Is it likely that the research the writer is planning to do will help them answer the question?

CONTINUED

2   Use a highlighter or number on the text where you can find the answers.

Has anything been left out? How would you improve it? Select two or three sentences that you could improve and rewrite them.

Figure 6.11: Will technology in healthcare benefit all?

Writing the main body of the essay

The main body of an essay will contain a number of paragraphs that explain your argument. Your paragraphs will need to address the issue you have chosen and the question you have asked. Your main body may include paragraphs on:

- causes and consequences of the issue
- counter arguments
- courses of action that can be taken
- possible solutions to the issue
- suggestions on what further research should be done.

Each body paragraph should begin with the main idea for the paragraph (the topic sentence); anyone reading your essay should be able to understand what the issue is and what your paragraph will focus on from the topic sentence. Your supporting sentences will then focus on different perspectives about the issue, or the causes and consequences of the issue, or the courses of action that might resolve the issue. You must support the points you make with evidence like relevant facts and figures, quotes from people, examples, or short anecdotes (stories).

In most subjects, you will find you are asked to write developed answers to questions, or to provide developed points. When you write your main body paragraphs, for example about courses of action, you should go beyond simply identifying or describing them and include details and explanation. This is called development. The extra details and explanation help your reader to understand properly the details of what you are proposing and how it would work. You should aim to answer any possible questions in your answer. Questions you could imagine could include: Who will do this? How? When? Why? What is the likely impact?

A good way of making the body of your essay read more fluently is to use connectives. Connectives are useful language markers to show your audience how you are shaping your argument. Examples of useful connectives are:

When to use it	Connectives
Sequencing	To begin, before, firstly, secondly, meanwhile, then, after, finally, penultimately, in conclusion, to conclude
Comparing	Similarly, like, as with, in the same way, equally, likewise
Contrasting	Alternatively, otherwise, whereas, on the other hand, unlike
Adding	Moreover, in addition, also, as well as, furthermore, to add on
Cause and effect	As a consequence, in effect, consequently, thus, therefore, so, because, but
Illustrating	For example, in the case of, for instance, such as, to show that

ACTIVITY 6.16

1 Read the following paragraph from an individual report on the topic of Transport, travel and tourism, about the consequences of mass tourism, and answer the questions that follow.

> Mass tourism continues to cause problems in host countries, including the destruction of local environments. This is continuing despite governments around the world trying to deal with the negative consequences of mass tourism, often by making new laws. According to the World Wildlife Fund (2015), the hunting and poaching of endangered species for ivory is increasing. This is particularly true of poaching rhino horn for medicine. Poaching gangs are becoming more organised. They are using more and more complex methods of trafficking, because of the potential profits they can obtain from trading ivory. Strict laws do not seem to be working to stop these gangs from carrying out this illegal and highly destructive practice. Furthermore, according to ECPAT International (2015), even though world leaders are committed to ending the exploitation of children, it is still a global consequence of mass tourism with hundreds of thousands of tourists involved in the abuse of people living in poverty. In addition, there is a noticeable worsening in the behaviour of some tourists, such as a lack of consideration for the local environment. Some governments find this difficult to prevent, despite their best efforts.
>
> **References:**
> World Wildlife Fund (2015) www.worldwildlife.org
> ECPAT (2015) www.ecpat.net

CONTINUED

a   What is the topic sentence?

b   Give an example of a supporting sentence.

c   How many connectives are used?

d   What evidence is presented?

e   Is all the evidence relevant to the first sentence? If not, could it be made relevant?

2   Do you think this text is a good example of a paragraph?
Explain your answer in your own written paragraph and share your thoughts with a partner.

Figure 6.12: Poaching species for ivory is increasing

ACTIVITY 6.17

Imagine you have decided on the following title for an essay:

'Is family life being affected by technology?'

1   Which of these two topic sentences do you think is better for the start of your essay and why?

   a   In this report, I am going to talk about technology.

   b   The last 20 years have seen immense changes in the way our lives have been and continue to be affected by technology.

2   Which of the following is the supporting sentence and which is the evidence for the first paragraph of your essay about whether family life is being affected by technology?

   a   In fact, according to a recent study, 8–18 year olds spend over seven hours a day using some form of media for entertainment, totalling over 50 hours per week.

   b   We are spending more time on our own than the rest of the family, inside on the computer and watching television, than we are outside in the fresh air.

3   Create a mind-map of other paragraphs for your essay. When you have finished, number your ideas on your mind-map to show what order they would go in. You do not have to use everything you have included in your mind-map but should aim for four or five strong ideas you would include.

TIP

Whenever you write an essay or a piece of coursework, you will be given a suggested word count. You must keep within that word count, of course. But if you write too little, you are likely to miss things out or provide too little evidence or explanation. If you write too much, you may repeat yourself or your writing may appear unstructured.

Writing the conclusion

The purpose of your conclusion is to summarise and make final comments on the ideas you have presented in your report or essay. It should not contain new evidence. The conclusion should be a strong answer to the question posed at the start of your report or essay and the last paragraph or two should be a justification of your personal perspective using the evidence you have presented throughout your report.

You can use this checklist for writing a conclusion:

- Write a new paragraph for your conclusion.

- Signpost to the reader that you are about to conclude by using words such as 'In conclusion', 'To summarise', 'Finally', 'To conclude'.

- Sum up your findings in answer to your research question.

- Give your personal perspective and justify it based on the evidence presented in your report.

- Only include evidence that you have given in the main part of your report.

- Check that your conclusion is a logical answer to the question you set out in the title of your report.

ACTIVITY 6.18

1   Read the following conclusion to the report about the consequences of mass tourism that you studied in Activity 6.16.

> Mass tourism is increasing, and we cannot prevent this because quicker and cheaper transportation means that people can, easily and cheaply, travel all over the world. What we can do is persuade governments and individuals that they are responsible for protecting the environment in areas where mass tourism is happening. We can make sure that tourists obey local rules and regulations. It is not acceptable that endangered species are threatened by poaching and hunting, so stronger action needs to be taken to stop this. Furthermore, without tourist demand for souvenirs made from materials obtained as a result of hunting and poaching, this practice would soon disappear as it would not be profitable enough to risk prison or large fines.
>
> I feel that it is clear that things are starting to change, and this will mean that sustainable tourism can be beneficial to an environment rather than harm it. More and more people are becoming aware of the need to protect endangered species, so access to certain areas is now heavily restricted. The protection of children is at the forefront of the international political agenda. Restrictions on groups of young people are now in place in some areas that previously suffered from violence and damage to the environment from alcohol-fuelled gangs.

2   Do you think this is a strong conclusion to a report about the impact of mass tourism? Give reasons for your answer.

3   Discuss your thoughts about the conclusion with a partner. Agree any changes that could be made to the conclusion, and write down how it could improve.

This conclusion summarises and makes final evaluative comments on the ideas presented. Although you do not have access to the rest of the report, you can see that the conclusion sums up the ideas and does not present new evidence. There is justification of a personal perspective using the evidence presented in this section of the report. You might also have been able to work out what the question was (‘*Can we protect local environments from the damage caused by mass tourism?*’).

Figure 6.13: Rusting 'love' locks, left by tourists, cause water pollution

Final steps in writing

Before handing in any written work you should make sure that your writing has structure, is accurate and explains the issue you are arguing. Questions to ask yourself include:

- Is the topic of each paragraph clear?

- Does each sentence in the paragraph help provide an understanding of the paragraph's topic?

- Does this sentence add to my argument, or does it just take up space?

- Does this sentence follow on from the sentence before and lead into the following sentence?

- Have I included evidence to support the argument I am making?

- Have I evaluated the sources of information I have used?

- Have I cited my sources and referenced them all in a reference list at the end of the report?

Revise your work until you are happy that you have presented your ideas clearly and effectively. Check your grammar; for example, make sure that every sentence contains a subject and a verb and that they agree with each other. Do a final proofread and correct any errors of spelling or punctuation.

SHOWCASING YOUR SKILLS

Communication

Create a presentation (either to an audience, on video, or via a web link meeting) of up to four minutes long, arguing your position on an issue you feel strongly about. You should first conduct research on your issue and then create a written script that explains your standpoint. You should use counter argument to strengthen the points you want to make.

You MUST:

- Practise what you are going to say and avoid reading from your script or notes.

- Make eye contact with the camera or audience.

- Speak clearly and not rush what you say.

- Have a presentation that is structured, easy to follow and cohesive.

- Answer the question and reflect on your own perspective and how it has been affected by your research, what you have learned and others' perspectives.

- Include a reference list for the sources you have used.

You SHOULD:

- Use appropriate gestures and pauses to emphasise your points.

- Use connectives to signpost the parts of your argument.

- Present a possible course of action for your issue and explain how it could be done and what impact it would have.

- Suggest further research that could be done or ideas that you think are missing from the research you have conducted.

You COULD:

- Engage the audience by asking questions, telling an anecdote or a joke.

- Use other visual aids or materials in your presentation.

- Ask for feedback after your presentation on what you did well and what could be improved.

Reflection on your showcase

Did you enjoy your presentation?

Write a few lines describing what went well.

Was your planning successful? How do you know?

What was difficult?

How could you improve things for next time?

Did this activity help you to improve your skills?

SUMMARY

In Chapter 6 you have been thinking about developing skills in reading, listening, speaking and writing. You have been creating effective arguments based on evidence and well-supported perspectives, and have been practising debating and presenting to an audience. You have considered how to present your researched material; in particular you have thought about a chosen issue and how to present your arguments, evidence and perspectives on this issue in a structured way.

REVIEW OF LEARNING

	I have learned about …	I need more practice with …
Using different reading strategies to help me take in information		
Listening actively and effectively		
Improving my speaking skills, including reading aloud and presenting to an audience		
Researching and presenting an argument, including presenting 'for' or 'against' a proposal in a debate		
Planning and writing an essay or report		
Presenting research including citations and references, arguments, evidence and perspectives		

> Chapter 7
Collaboration

LEARNING INTENTIONS

In this chapter you will:

- Practise working collaboratively, including making decisions as a team, considering roles and responsibilities and resolving disagreements

- Plan a team project

- Agree on an issue for a team project to address

- Divide up the research for your project and share your findings

- Agree on a project aim and action

- Explain your project

- Work as a team on an action for a team project.

Note: where examples of student work are provided, these have been written by our authors.

In this chapter you will be working on your teamworking skills. You will have the chance to collaborate in a range of different ways. You will practise sharing ideas and research and planning as a team so that you are able to work effectively to achieve the aims of a team project and carry out an action. As you have seen already in the course, the key to successful teamwork is communication, being clear about your own ideas and feelings and listening carefully to others and taking their viewpoints into consideration.

You will explore material relating to the topics of Water, food and agriculture, Environment, pollution and conservation, and Health and wellbeing. You will also be able to investigate and research an issue for a team project.

Figure 7.1: Collaboration can help teams work effectively

BEFORE YOU START

This chapter builds on the pair work and group work you have been doing throughout previous activities in this book and the teamwork activity you carried out in 'Showcasing your skills' at the end of Chapter 2 when you carried out a short project with a team. Look back at this and the list of skills shown below. For each, write down when you have most recently done this and how confident you feel with the skill. You will be developing and building on them further in this chapter:

- share ideas with other people

- listen to other people's ideas

- share out tasks with other people

- perform a task alongside others.

7.1 Working collaboratively

We have seen that Cambridge Global Perspectives develops your independent learning skills. It also enables you to work with others. You can do this in class in pairs and in small groups and teams. Working in groups can be a helpful way of tackling large or complicated tasks where having more people helps to spread the workload. Problem solving can sometimes be easier with more people to think about any issue and come up with solutions.

You will be able to use the skills of teamwork in other subject areas. They will also be useful for future learning and when you are employed. In fact, many employers look for the ability to be able to work in teams as one of their key requirements when they are interviewing people for work. Being able to work as a team member is important in sport, at school and in the workplace. Working well in a team is an advantage that many employers look for. Think of an activity which is done as a team and why this works better than it being done as an individual.

You probably thought about a sport like football or basketball. The main reason why these are team sports is that each individual brings something to the team to enable the team as a whole to be successful in its aim – winning the game or match (Figure 7.2).

Figure 7.2: Individuals contribute to team success in sports like basketball

> **DISCUSSION**
>
> Discuss with a partner why you think teamwork is important. Does your partner share your viewpoint?

When discussing why teamwork is important, you might have decided that teamwork teaches you to work together towards an aim or goal. Other people can often think of things you might have forgotten or missed. It is usually more interesting to work with others as they bring different perspectives and ideas to the task. You do not have to do everything on your own, so you can achieve more, faster. Collaboration (working with others) and communication are required for effective teamwork. You will develop these skills as you progress through the Cambridge IGCSE and O Level Global Perspectives course.

ACTIVITY 7.01

1   Read the following statements about collaborating on a team project and put them in order of importance, starting with the most important:

   a   All members of the team must understand the aims of the project.

   b   Team members must all be clear about the plans and about members' roles and responsibilities.

   c   Team members must support each other and appreciate each other's perspectives.

   d   Each team member's thoughts should be listened to by others.

   e   Each team member should take part in the team's decisions and actions.

   f   Team members should be appreciated as individuals.

   g   The team works together to solve any problems with good communication skills.

2   Share your order of importance with a partner. Did they choose the same order as you? Discuss any differences and agree a final order that you are both happy with. You may need to compromise a little.

3   Share your agreed order with your group and discuss and come to a compromise about the order you can all agree on.

Using empathy when working with others

When working in a team, or indeed in any dealings with other people (or even when you are simply trying to understand different people's perspectives), the ability to feel and show **empathy** is a great asset. Empathy means that not only do you listen to and try to understand someone's ideas or feelings, you also try to share their perspective and how they might be feeling or thinking. Often, people will confuse empathy with sympathy, but empathy is more challenging to achieve and involves careful listening and thinking. Empathy is useful in many types of situations, particularly where there are challenging circumstances such as a conflict of ideas or personalities. Empathy allows space for understanding on both sides and can help move a situation on in a positive way.

As with all the skills within this book, empathy is one that can be developed. Being able to empathise will help you to work well in a team, get the most out of your Cambridge IGCSE and O Level Global Perspectives course and be able to build and maintain close friendships and develop strong communities.

> **KEY TERM**
>
> **empathy:** the experience of understanding and sharing another person's feelings from their perspective. You place yourself 'in their shoes' and imagine what they are feeling.

TIP

You will explore empathy further in Chapter 8, Section 8.3.

Making decisions collaboratively

When working on a team project, your team will need to make decisions. Everyone should be involved and know what is going on. Teamwork requires everyone to take part and support the teamwork. If one person makes all the decisions or does all the work, that is not collaborative and other team members will not be happy.

Some team decisions will be easy to make without much thought. Others need much more careful consideration to discuss the possible outcomes before making a decision. Figure 7.3 gives eight questions to think about when making a decision as a team.

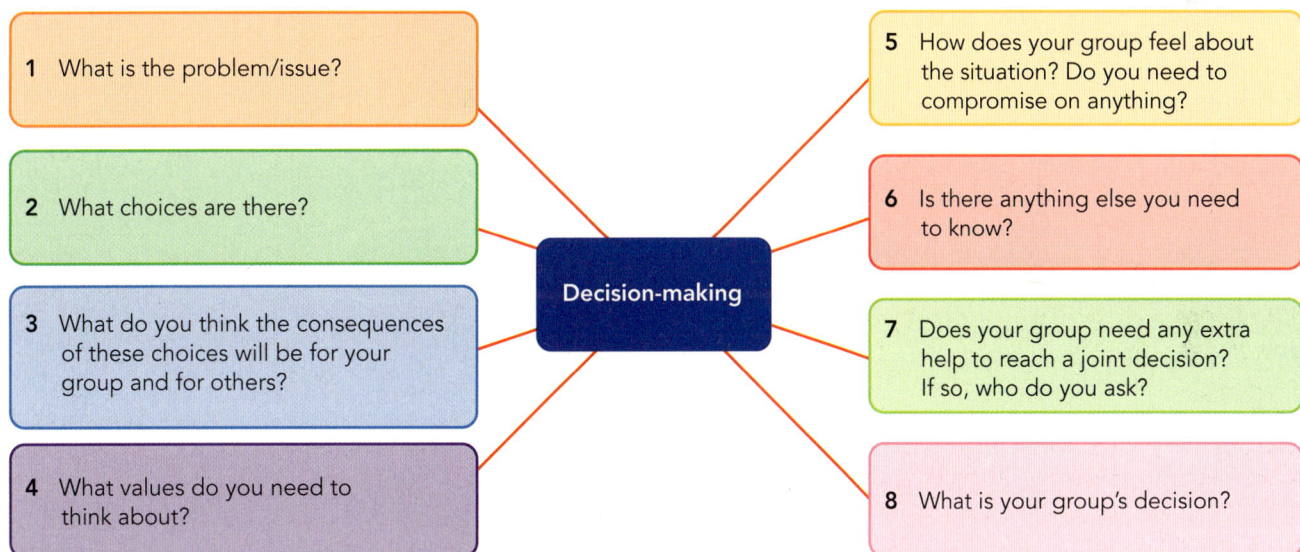

1   What is the problem/issue?

2   What choices are there?

3   What do you think the consequences of these choices will be for your group and for others?

4   What values do you need to think about?

Decision-making

5   How does your group feel about the situation? Do you need to compromise on anything?

6   Is there anything else you need to know?

7   Does your group need any extra help to reach a joint decision? If so, who do you ask?

8   What is your group's decision?

Figure 7.3: Decision-making questions

After considering the decision-making questions in Figure 7.3, the team will also need to make a group decision. Reaching an agreement can be difficult. You will need to listen with empathy to your team members' opinions and you might have to compromise on what you want personally so the group can come to a consensus and make a final decision.

Once a decision has been made, you can then evaluate it by answering the questions: 'Do you think your team has made the right decision? Why/why not?' You can disagree with the decision that your team has made but still be able to work successfully with the group. When you evaluate decisions it is useful to explain what you would have done differently and what consequences this would have had.

DISCUSSION

Imagine you are walking along the street and a homeless person asks you for money. In a small group, discuss with a partner your answers to the eight questions in Figure 7.3 for this situation. Can you reach a decision that you all agree on? Why/why not?

Figure 7.4: What would you do if a homeless person asked you for money?

REFLECTION

Think about a time when you think you or a team you were a member of might have made the wrong decision. Work through the eight decision-making questions in Figure 7.3 and reflect on why this decision might have been wrong. What would you have changed?

Often there is no one right choice and you might think that very few decisions are totally wrong. Even if you feel you or your team made the wrong decision at the time, you might be able to make up for it if a similar situation arises again. After the discussion with your group about giving money to a homeless person, did you think about changing your decisions or not? Give reasons for your answer.

ACTIVITY 7.03

1   Read through each of the following issues with your group and work with your group to come to a decision:

a   Should your group ask the school to buy Fairtrade chocolate bars that can be sold for a school fundraising project, rather than the normal chocolate even though the Fairtrade chocolate is a little more expensive and fundraising money received will not be as much?

TIP

Decision-making can be a process, not just a single decision. We might come up with different ideas when we spend more time thinking about our decision, or change our minds when we find out new information. This is the same whether you are making individual decisions or taking decisions as a team.

b Should schools send students to travel abroad by plane on study vacations when there are plenty of beautiful and suitable locations in your own country?

2 For each one, work through the eight questions in Figure 7.3, applying them to the issue. Write down your decisions when you have come to an agreement. Share your decisions with another group.

Deciding on roles and responsibilities for team projects and group activities

It will get your teamwork off to a good start if at the beginning of the project you focus on team roles and their responsibilities. Everyone in the team is still responsible for contributing overall to the team project or activity, but these roles help keep the team on track and identify problem areas early. You may decide to use the roles suggested in Figure 7.5, or to allocate other roles and responsibilities – the decision is up to you and your teammates.

A. The leader

I am the leader. I help the team to be successful by keeping it on task and on track.

I am responsible for making sure that everyone in the team understands what needs to be done and carries out their role.

B. The recorder

I am the recorder. I collect and share the information we discuss and I keep a record of the work we have done, and of key ideas. In addition I keep copies of each member's work.

I also prepare the team explanation and keep evidence of the action.

C. The encourager

I am the encourager. I listen carefully to other team members and share ideas.

I try to help when anyone gets stuck with their work and suggest where they could get other help or resources.

D. The checker

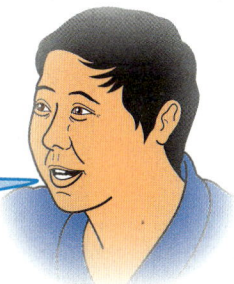

I am the checker. I make sure that everyone understands the decisions we have made and what work needs to be done.

I also check that everyone is on track to finish their work on time so that the project can be completed by the deadline.

Figure 7.5: Team roles

DISCUSSION

1   Take a few minutes to think about the following: Which of these the roles shown in Figure 7.5 do you think would suit you? Why? Are there some aspects of different roles that suit you? Can you think of any other useful roles, or any other way of dividing up a team workload? Make a note of your ideas to share with others.

2   Now, with a partner or in a group, discuss which roles each of you might take in a team project. Share your ideas of other possible roles or other ways of dividing a team workload. Do you agree on which roles would suit each of you? Should you consider sharing some of the roles if you have different strengths?

TIP

You can take different roles and responsibilities at different times. You do not have to take the same role every time. There is nothing to stop you adopting different roles for different team projects or group activities.

Resolving disagreements

When you are working in a team with others, you may find that the team dynamics, disagreements and arguments cause problems and get in the way of working together well. Sometimes you may have personality clashes, or some people think they are doing more work than others. These are all reasons why you may need to deal with difficult interactions when you are engaged in teamwork. Some ways that you can resolve disagreements in your team include:

1   Empathise: listen carefully. Try to understand your teammate's viewpoint and the decisions they have made. It does not mean you have to agree. What you are trying to do is show you understand how they feel and how they are thinking. You might try repeating back what you have heard to check with the other person that you have understood them.

2   Give team members responsibilities: this creates a shared purpose for the team and allows everyone working on the project to know what they are doing, why they are doing it, and how their responsibility fits into the end project. Negotiating changes to responsibilities can also help to get a team back on track after a disagreement.

3   Look for possible solutions: problem solving can resolve arguments by giving teams a chance to think creatively and discuss possible solutions together. It is important to practise empathy when discussing the ways your project could move forward.

ACTIVITY 7.04

1   The following table sets out four different team problems.

Team 1 is getting annoyed that one of the members, Hannah, doesn't seem to be doing the same amount of work as the others in the group.	**Team 2** likes to work individually and does not like to share what they have been working on with each other. They have repeated the same research and wasted a lot of time. Their team project isn't going very well.
Team 3 has decided to use a group chat app to collaborate instead of meeting face to face. Two team members do not have their own mobile phones. One team member does not have a computer or a mobile phone.	**Team 4** was assigned by the teacher. They do not know each other well and have never spoken to each other before.

With a partner, discuss how you could deal with the difficult situations in a team, using the resolution methods above to solve the various problems.

2   Note down your ideas for solving the problems. Ask another pair how they solved the problems.

3   With your partner, try to come up with some rules for working in a team so that these situations do not occur when you are doing teamwork.

7.2 Planning a team project

When working on a team project, you will need to make decisions such as:

- the issue that your project will address
- what information you need to know (find out)
- which resources you are going to use (websites, books, actual people, etc.)
- what your project aim and team action will be
- who is going to do what, when and why.

Having a clear plan will help you to make these decisions together and to work well as a team.

ACTIVITY 7.05

Put the following steps into the most suitable order for completing a team project:

a   Choose team members.

b   Give reasons for the choice of topic.

c   Identify team roles.

d   Choose the global topic.

e   Identify tasks to be undertaken.

f   Decide on the action you will take.

g   Write an explanation of your project.

h   Match tasks to team member roles.

i   Carry out tasks (including secondary and primary research to gather different perspectives).

j   Decide on the aim of the project.

k   Identify the time frame for the completion of tasks.

You don't have to use a template to plan your team project, but it might help you to draw one up.

Figure 7.6 shows an example plan for a team project. Evaluate it by identifying the following:

- strengths
- limitations
- possible improvements.

Having clear tasks and time frames for completing them are important to keep your project running smoothly. You might also wish to assign roles or people to certain tasks, as in the plan in Figure 7.6. Taking time to plan out the activities your group needs to complete at the beginning of the project can help avoid problems later. Some of the common pitfalls are:

- Taking too long to decide on what you want to do.
- Not having enough research or not having research that considers multiple perspectives.
- Not being clear on who is doing what task.
- Not keeping a good record of sources and notes.
- Not organising time effectively and leaving the biggest tasks until the end.

Project plan

Aim: To raise awareness about women's health issues

Action: Publish a news article on a Facebook page

Team members: Maha, Rula, Rita, Rosa

Sources of information
Secondary:
World Health Organization website
United Nations website
Women's health websites from different countries

Primary:
Interviews with medical staff at the local hospital - recorded interviews
Questionnaires completed by students from other countries - email, Skype

Task	Who?	Time frame
Find information about women's health issues globally	Maha and Rita	1 week
Find information about women's health issues nationally	Rula and Rosa	1 week
Contact hospital to organise interviews with medical staff at the local hospital	All	1 week
Write up findings from recorded interviews from the hospital	Maha, Rula	1 week
Design questionnaire and email to group of students in another country (ask Miss D for contact details)	Rita and Rosa	1 week
Analyse and summarise findings from questionnaire	Rita	1 week
Start to organise research findings. Has enough research been done?	Maha and Rula	1 week
Write an explanation for the teacher of what we are going to do	Rula and Rosa	1 week
Write news article (Action) and evaluate group decisions	Maha and Rita	1 week

Figure 7.6: Project plan

7.3 Agreeing on an issue to work on together

To start working together on a team project, you will have to agree on what you are going to do and why. You might want to try to do some good in your local area. If so, before you can decide on the specific aim of your project, you will first need to agree on the local issue you will be trying to help out on. You will have to identify what issues there are in your local area and then – as a team – agree on one issue to work on.

You should find out what different people think about this issue and what solutions have been tried to deal with this issue in different places.

A good place to start is to think of your local area, town or city and list some of the problems you see around you.

TIP

When you are writing what your issue is and what you would like to focus on, try not to make your definition too broad. For example: 'Poverty' does not say how this issue affects your local area. Something like: 'We are looking at education poverty in our local area and are focusing on what is the minimum amount of school equipment needed for all students to participate' is clear, measurable and allows space to look at other places in comparison.

ACTIVITY 7.06

Practise exploring issues. Take a look at Figures 7.7 to 7.10 and complete the tasks that follow.

Figure 7.7: Issue A

Figure 7.8: Issue B

Figure 7.9: Issue C

Figure 7.10: Issue D

> **CONTINUED**
>
> 1 Look at Figure 7.7 and answer the following questions:
>
>   **a** What is the main issue? What other connected issues are there?
>
>   **b** What are the causes and consequences of this issue?
>
>   **c** Who is it an issue for? Who else might also be affected?
>
>   **d** What can be done to improve the issue?
>
>   Share your answers with a partner.
>
> 2 Now with your partner look at Figure 7.8 and answer the same questions.
>
>   Share your thoughts with your team.
>
> 3 In your team, look at Figures 7.9 and 7.10 and answer the same questions for each.
>
>   As a group discuss the issues that fit these pictures.
>
> 4 Now, individually, take a few minutes to think quietly about any issues you have noticed in your local area, town or city. Write down two or three ideas.
>
> 5 Share your ideas with your team.

When you have identified and considered a number of individual issues that you might be able to investigate as a group, the next stage is to narrow them down in order to find one which you can all agree on. One way of doing this is to look for similarities between the different issues and to group them together.

> **ACTIVITY 7.07**
>
> Work as a group.
>
> 1 On a large piece of paper, draw a mind-map. Write your chosen issue in the centre and add on the problems and ideas that come from that issue. Make sure you include everyone's ideas. If more than one of you had the same idea, write the number of people who thought of the same one next to that idea. Try to group similar thoughts together.
>
> 2 When all your ideas have been mapped out on the sheet of paper, take a look at the topics for Cambridge IGCSE and O Level Global Perspectives and write the topics next to the ideas they link to.
>
> 3 When you have completed your mind-map, take a look at other groups' mind-maps and see whether they have come up with any different ideas, or have linked problems with different topics. Your group can amend or add to your mind-map.

CONTINUED

4   Now – as a team – you need to narrow down your mind-map options to discuss and agree on a problem to work on by deciding what the strongest ideas are. You can use this decision as a base for what your team project will be on. You will research it first to decide: Is there enough information available on this issue? If there is, you can select this as your issue to work on and then you will plan an action to make a difference. If there is not, you will need to go back to your mind-map and select another problem to investigate. When you think your team is ready, check with your teacher whether the issue will be appropriate and acceptable.

7.4 Dividing up research and sharing findings

When completing research for a project as a team, it is often sensible to divide up the work so that each team member carries out some individual research.

For your project, every team member should initially research one aspect of your issue and/or a different perspective on that issue. Information could include facts and figures about different aspects of your chosen issue and information about solutions tried in different places. Perspectives could be from people who are affected by your issue, people who might be able to do something about it or who are working in the area, experts who might know about the issue or people from other places who might be able to tell you about solutions they have used.

Plan out who will research what. Then, when you have all done your research, you will share all your findings together to help you plan your project. This research will help you all to understand the issue better and to work out what might be a good course of action to take as a team.

> **TIP**
>
> When reflecting later on your experience of your team project, don't forget to include your thoughts on your initial personal research.

ACTIVITY 7.08

In your group, discuss how to divide up the research for your project. Each one of you should research a different aspect or a different perspective. (You will share your findings with each other so that you can decide what the best action could be to help make a difference.)

1   Draw up a list of the research that is needed, and make a note of who will do what research.

2   Decide if you will interview people for some of the research. Decide who you might interview.

CONTINUED

3   Decide how many of the team members will interview people. (Remember that different team members should interview different people or ask different questions so that you do individual research.) Make sure you follow the rules set down by your teacher and school for checking whether the interview is allowed. Also check whether the people you want to interview will be willing or able to be interviewed.

4   Agree on questions for any interviews/surveys/questionnaires.

5   Agree a time limit when everyone will bring their research to the team for discussion. You do not need to do a lot of research, just enough to help you all to decide what to do as your action.

6   Choose a spokesperson to share your issue and research plan with the rest of the class.

7   Share with the class.

When agreeing to take on individual research tasks, make sure that you are able to do what have agreed to do. Also make sure you have everyone's agreement (teacher, parents, interviewees) if you are going to carry out interviews. You should always go with at least one other person.

Figure 7.11: Research can involve interviewing people

ACTIVITY 7.09

As individuals, carry out your research and be ready to share it with your team. Make notes of your findings and your sources as you will need those later on to reflect on your project. Before you meet the rest of your team, summarise your findings if you have a lot of information. Note the main points you found out and be ready to share them without going into too much detail.

Be sure to do your agreed research promptly, so that everyone's research is completed in time to share your findings.

ACTIVITY 7.10

As a team, meet together to share your findings.

1 Agree the order in which you will share your research, and how you will share it.

2 Each team member should then share their results with the team. Make notes of each other's main findings and discuss what you have learned.

3 Then decide whether you have enough information and ideas to go ahead with your project. If not, work out what more you need to know. Organise one or two of you to find out extra information if you really need more.

7.5 Deciding on a project aim and action

When you are happy that you have enough information to know that your chosen issue is a good one for your team to work on, you can decide as a team what your project aim will be. For example, you might decide to take some action aiming to help directly with the issue.

Agree your aim and all make a note of that. Check with your teacher whether this is a realistic aim for you to achieve in the time you have to do your work.

When you have decided what your project aim is, you will need to decide on an action to take that will achieve your aim.

The action you choose to carry out should be suitable for the project's aim. It should allow you to communicate your research into different perspectives. It could be any of the following (or something else you think of):

- a practical activity to make a difference directly

- a campaign or event to raise money/collect items for a local charity or organisation that helps with the issue

- a mural or wall art exploring possible solutions and their consequences.

Specific suggestions for your action include creating:

- an information leaflet or brochure to hand out to people

- a video clip to show to an audience

- a series of photos, for example showing a fundraising event that you organised and took part in

- a poem or a song which you perform live or produce as a video or audio clip

- a web page directed at a group of people

- lessons you plan and teach, perhaps to a younger audience and in another school

- cartoons with captions published or shown to others
- a model or design for a solution that is shown or explained to others.

The action is a chance for your team to show creativity.

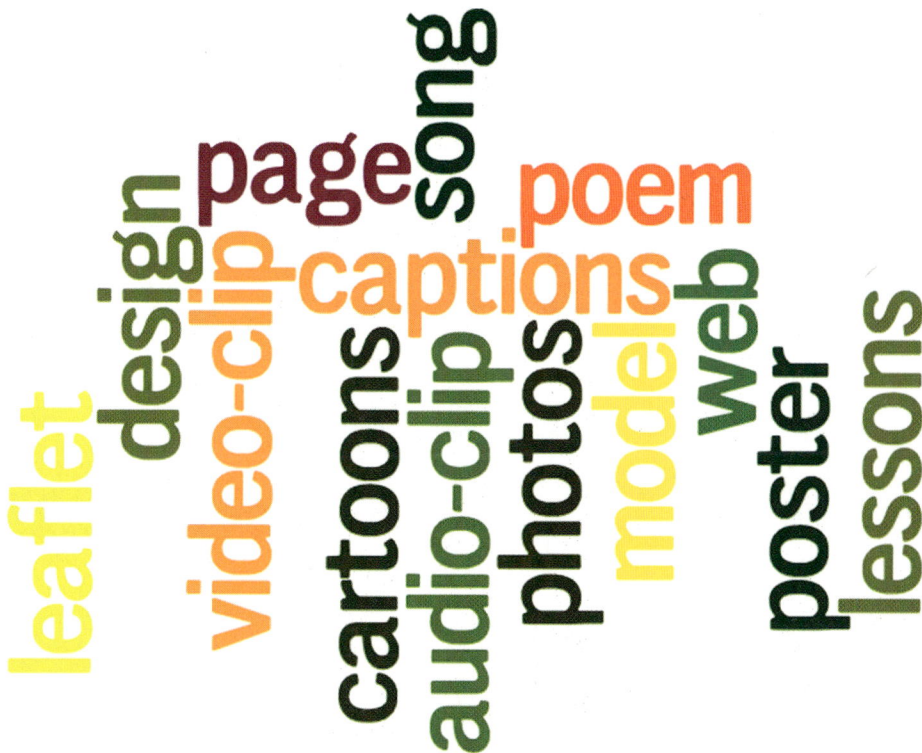

Figure 7.12: There are many creative possibilities for your action

ACTIVITY 7.11

1   As a group, decide on a suitable aim for a project related to the issue that you agreed to focus on in Activity 7.07 or subsequently.

2   Now decide what action you would like to take in order to achieve your aim.

3   Consider the following:

   a   Who will be responsible for what task? How will you decide the roles and responsibilities? How will your group monitor the process and the progress?

   b   How will you measure whether you have been successful in achieving your aim? Will your action have an impact in the long term and change the way people do things?

   c   How are you going to provide your teacher with evidence of your action? This could include photos of the action, video, presentation, documents such as leaflets and results of surveys.

7.6 Explaining your project

Following on from your group meeting and discussions in Activities 7.9 and 7.10, you should have a clear idea of what you are intending to do as a team to help make a difference to the issue you've agreed upon. This will include what each person's role is and what they have researched. You should now be able to provide a clear explanation of your project, outlining what you are going to do and the reasons why.

Your explanation should outline your project aims and your plan of action, including:

- who will do what

- how you will collect evidence of your action

- how you will measure the success of your action.

You can amend your explanation/plan as you go along, if things change or the team realises there is a better action to take, or something will not work.

ACTIVITY 7.12

1   In pairs, consider the following aim and action for a team project on the topic of Water, food and agriculture:

  - Project aim: To persuade young people of the importance of a varied diet by trying foods from different cultures.

  - Action: Create a weekly menu suggesting a variety of healthy dishes and snacks from around the world.

2   Look at Figure 7.13 and as a pair decide whether you think it meets the project aim.

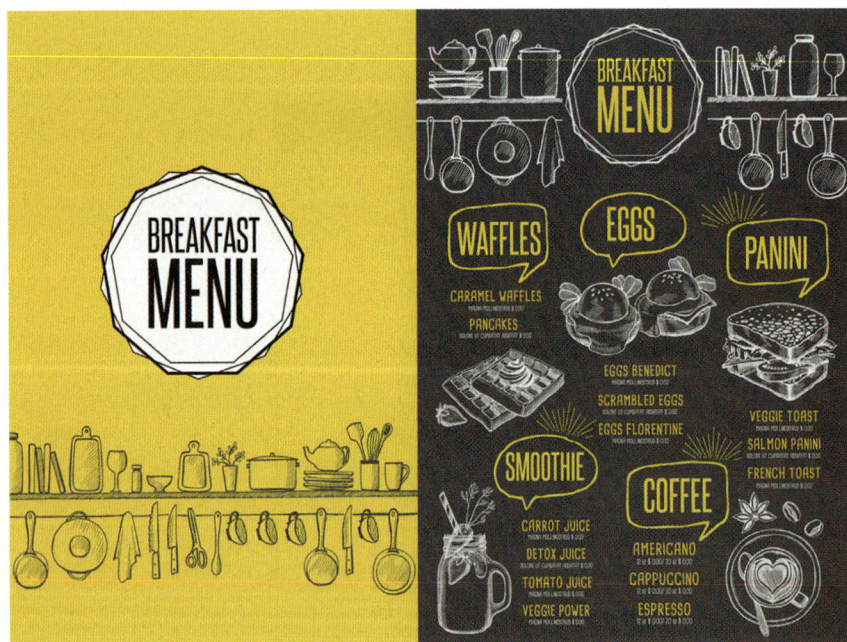

Figure 7.13: Menu recommending options for breakfast

CONTINUED

3   Could you and your partner think of anything to improve the menu, or any additional action to make sure that you achieve the aim of the project? Note down your ideas to share later with the rest of your group.

4   Now consider this sample explanation for the same project aim.

For our team project, we were interested in the celebrations we have throughout the year that are centred on food. We discovered by talking to students in lower grade classes that they eat a lot of fast food, which is very unhealthy as it is full of sugar and salt which makes us fat. We wanted to persuade Grade 7 students in our school of the benefits of trying different types of food and the enjoyment they could get from experiencing foods from other cultures. We allocated team roles to ensure that we could complete the project in the time frame we set ourselves. Each one of us was allocated a role by the self-appointed team leader. As well as this role, each one of us was responsible for researching at least one other culture or contacting a person from another country so that we could get together and share the information we found out before designing our series of menus.

We contacted other schools that are studying Cambridge IGCSE and O Level Global Perspectives in a few different countries: Indonesia, Australia and India. Then we produced a series of menus showing the healthy foods enjoyed by these cultures. Our action shows that Indian food is generally healthy as there are a variety of vegetarian dishes that are eaten regularly. Indonesians prefer pork in soy sauce, pork rice, cakes and tarts. Usually, there are two buffet tables, one with pork dishes and one with halal food, like grilled fish, for Muslim guests. In Australia, seafood and salads are very popular. Australians also eat a lot of meat, but it is lean and often grilled.

CONTINUED

5   With a partner, draw up a checklist to determine whether the explanation above includes:

- what the team has agreed

- a mention of each person's role and what they have researched

- an explanation of what the team is going to do and why

- an outline of the project aims

- the team's plan of action, including:

    - who will do what

    - information about how they will collect evidence of your action

    - information about how they will measure the success of your action.

Use your checklist to check that everything is included in the explanation above. Is anything missing? Is anything included in the explanation that is not required?

6   Do you and your partner think that this project achieved its aim? Did the explanation convince you that it did? Could you think of any other way of achieving the aim that would be more effective? Share your thoughts with your group.

ACTIVITY 7.13

1   In your group, discuss and write an explanation of the team project you have been working on in the previous activities. One of you can collect everyone's ideas and do the actual word-processing, but all of you should be involved and agree the finished document. Keep things short and direct so that your explanation is clear.

2   Use your checklist from Activity 7.12 to make sure that you have included everything.

3   When you have completed your team project explanation, share it with another group and read theirs.

4   Make any suggestions for improvements and note down any suggestions the other group gives you.

5   Make any changes that you feel are necessary before you start to work in your group on your action.

SHOWCASING YOUR SKILLS

Collaboration

By now your team should have agreed on an issue to address as a team, your team project aim and the action you are going to take to achieve your aim.

Your team should have agreed on how you will carry out your action, who will do what and when everything will be completed.

Make sure that you have decided in advance how you will measure the success of your action in achieving your project aim.

Now work together to make any materials you need and to plan and carry out your event or other action.

Your teacher will give you a deadline to work to.

Remember to collect evidence of your action that you can present to your teacher when you have completed your work.

Reflection on the showcase

Did you enjoy working collaboratively?

Write a few lines describing what went well.

Was the action successful? How do you know?

What was difficult?

How could you improve things for next time?

Did this activity help you to develop your collaboration skills?

SUMMARY

In Chapter 7 you have been thinking about and practising collaboration skills.

You have looked at some examples of how you can work collaboratively, including making decisions as a team, allocating roles and responsibilities, and resolving disagreements. You have practised working as a team, including selecting an issue to work on, agreeing a project aim and action, allocating roles and responsibilities, explaining your project and carrying out your action.

REVIEW OF LEARNING

	I have learned about …	I need more practice with …
Working collaboratively, including making decisions, agreeing responsibilities and resolving disagreements		
Planning a team project		
Agreeing on an issue for the team to address		
Sharing research		
Agreeing on an aim for a team project and on an action that the team will carry out		
Working as a team to explain our team project		
Working together to carry out a team project		

› Chapter 8
Reflection

LEARNING INTENTIONS

By the end of this chapter you will be able to:

- Understand different reflective learning strategies

- Reflect objectively on different perspectives

- Reflect on others' perspectives with empathy

- Justify your own perspective using evidence and reasoning

- Reflect on the experience of working in a team.

Note: where examples of student work are provided, these have been written by our authors.

In this chapter you will be investigating different strategies to help you reflect and sharing your group learning with the whole class. You will reflect on different perspectives, trying to keep an open mind and trying to understand others' situations. You will carry out some role-plays, imagining yourself in someone else's place. You will give a presentation to the class and take part in a class debate. You will also learn how to capture your reflections in a reflective paper. These activities will help you to justify your own perspective while comparing it with those of others, and to reflect these in writing.

The topics you will be exploring are Sport and recreation, Health and wellbeing, Education for all and Poverty and inequality.

BEFORE YOU START

Think about the reflection you have done during this course. During each chapter you have been invited to reflect on ideas and information and on your own experiences and to relate your learning to these. You have also been invited to reflect on your own skills and learning at the end of each chapter.

1   Look back at some of your reflections.

2   Write down which reflection has helped you most with your learning and at least one reason why.

3   Attempt to write your own definition of reflection.

8.1 Reflective learning strategies

As you have seen throughout this course, reflection is a good way of 'learning from experience'. Reflection allows us to analyse experiences and events so that we can continue to do what works and change anything that does not work or does not go well. Reflection also allows us to consider the reasons things did or did not work. Reflecting on experiences helps us to remember them better and for longer, and allows us to develop personally and professionally. Reflection helps us to analyse and discuss our feelings or ideas with others, so that we can look at them from other points of view.

Reflection is a key skill for your study of Cambridge Global Perspectives. After you have completed an activity, you think about what you did, and what happened, and decide what you would do differently next time. After you have completed a project as part of a team, you can write reflectively about it, sharing your experiences of the project so that your reader knows what happened and understands your thoughts on the whole experience. In this reflective writing, you can share your thoughts on the benefits and challenges of working in a team and your own performance as a team member. You can reflect on the strengths and limitations of what you have produced as a result of the project in achieving your aim. You can also explain what you have learned from your research and different perspectives you have explored.

Reflection is important when working individually too. For example, when writing a report that examines different perspectives, you can reflect on your research findings in the light of others' perspectives. You can also use reflection to explain to your reader how your own perspective has been affected by your research.

Reflection is also a useful life-long skill to help you make better choices and decisions. If you are a reflective learner, you are more likely to be more of an independent learner, someone who is **self-aware** and motivated to continue learning.

KEY TERM

self-aware: aware of your own character, feelings, motives and desires.

Figure 8.1: Reflections can be about things that happen externally or internally

ACTIVITY 8.01

Choose one of the four different reflective learning strategies which are presented below. If you are working as a class, different groups can choose a strategy each.

Once you have chosen the strategy you want to try out, follow the prompts below which will guide you through it. Once you have done this, be ready to explain the strategy and your thoughts on how effective it is.

Group A – Strategy 1: The 'four prompts' strategy

To develop your reflection skills further, you can use the 'four prompts' strategy. This strategy can be used for experiences and for activities that involve researching information, either by reading or by listening.

Four prompts to develop your reflections:

- Identify one important idea, piece of information or research finding that you learned while doing an activity.

- Ask yourself why you think this idea, piece of information or research finding is important.

- Think about how what you have learned connects with your own ideas.

- Consider the questions you now want answers to and why these questions are important to you.

CONTINUED

1 Practise using this strategy:

a Read the text below about anti-doping policy in sport.

b Answer the four prompts.

c Record your answers.

d Share your answers with a partner.

e Add any further thoughts to your answers after discussion with your partner.

Press Release

BEIJING, Feb 18 (Reuters) – The World Anti-Doping Agency (WADA) on Friday accused the Court of Arbitration for Sport (CAS) of ignoring the world anti-doping code when it upheld the Russian anti-doping authorities' decision to lift the provisional suspension of Russian teenage figure skater Kamila Valieva at the Beijing Olympics.

CAS ruled on Monday that Valieva should be allowed to compete in the women's competition despite having failed a drug test at her national championships last December.

The result was only revealed on Feb. 8, a day after Valieva helped the Russian Olympic Committee win the team event at the Beijing Games.

… on Friday, CAS said it agreed with the Disciplinary Committee (DADC) of the Russian Anti-Doping Agency's argument that the 15-year-old Valieva, being a 'protected person' (i.e. an under-16 athlete), did not need to meet the usual standards to prove that she did not willingly take the banned heart drug she tested positive for.

… Valieva's defence had argued that the positive test resulted from a mix-up with her grandfather's heart drug, trimetazidine.

"In the DADC's opinion, in fact, the Athlete could have consumed a product which has been contaminated by the drugs used in her inner circle," CAS continued.

That explanation did not satisfy, WADA, who said that a 'protected person' should not be treated differently as far as provisional suspensions are concerned.

"In effect, by making this award, the CAS Panel has re-written the Code to say that mandatory provisional suspensions for 'protected persons' shall now be considered as optional provisional suspensions," WADA said in a statement.

CONTINUED

> … "This re-writing of the Code, which would apparently allow `protected persons' to continue competing after testing positive for non-specified substances without any clarification of the circumstances, risks undermining the integrity of sporting competition and the confidence of athletes that they are competing on a level playing field."
>
> *Source: Court of Arbitration for Sport ignored anti-doping code in Valieva ruling, says WADA (www.reuters.com, adapted)*

2   Now share the answers with the rest of your group. As a group be ready to explain this strategy to the rest of the class. Did you find it helpful? Would you use this strategy yourselves?

Group B – Strategy 2: The 'five key questions' strategy

The 'five key questions' strategy is a useful, fairly quick way of reflecting. By answering the five key questions in Figure 8.2, you describe what happened and reflect on the experience in a meaningful way.

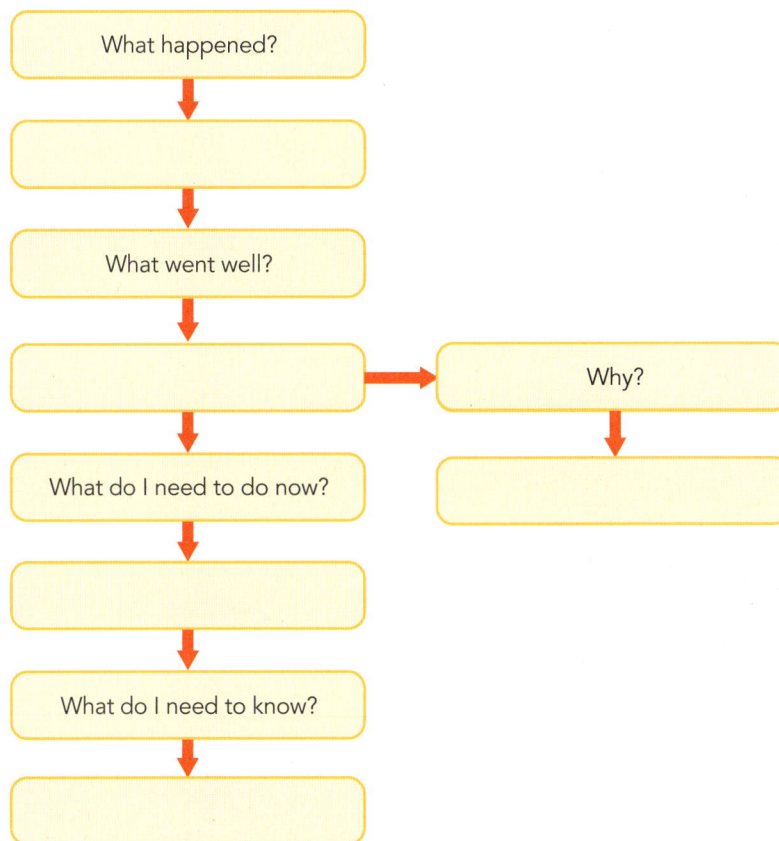

```
┌──────────────────────┐
│   What happened?     │
└──────────────────────┘
           │
           ▼
┌──────────────────────┐
│                      │
└──────────────────────┘
           │
           ▼
┌──────────────────────┐
│   What went well?    │
└──────────────────────┘
           │
           ▼
┌──────────────────────┐        ┌──────────────────────┐
│                      │───────▶│        Why?          │
└──────────────────────┘        └──────────────────────┘
           │                               │
           ▼                               ▼
┌──────────────────────┐        ┌──────────────────────┐
│ What do I need to    │        │                      │
│     do now?          │        └──────────────────────┘
└──────────────────────┘
           │
           ▼
┌──────────────────────┐
│                      │
└──────────────────────┘
           │
           ▼
┌──────────────────────┐
│ What do I need to    │
│     know?            │
└──────────────────────┘
           │
           ▼
┌──────────────────────┐
│                      │
└──────────────────────┘
```

Figure 8.2: The 'five key questions' strategy

CONTINUED

1   Read the blog entry below and identify which part of the blog answers each of the five questions in Figure 8.2.

> For our team project we decided to create and deliver a presentation to make other people aware of the problem of global warming. We wanted to start with Grade 7 students and inform them that they too had a responsibility to help slow down global warming. We knew that they were not aware of the things they could do, so we wanted to show them how every individual can help in some way.

✓ We had a group meeting and shared our initial ideas about what should be in the presentation. This initial brainstorming discussion went well as everyone seemed prepared to contribute their ideas.

✓ However, I was sometimes a bit reluctant to voice my opinion as I didn't feel that I had done enough research and I thought the others in my group would think my suggestions were silly.

✓ I feel that, before our next meeting, I need to do some more research so that I am knowledgeable about the main causes of global warming.

✓ I will ask Ms Chad if she can suggest a couple of good websites I could look at that focus on the causes of global warming. Then I will be able to think about possible solutions and be ready with my ideas at our next team meeting.

2   Now discuss the answers to the five key questions with your group. As a group be ready to explain this strategy to the rest of the class. Did you find it helpful? Would you use this strategy yourselves?

CONTINUED

Group C – Strategy 3: The 'five stages' strategy

The 'five stages' strategy helps you to reflect on an experience in a structured way as follows:

A   Look back and describe what happened: the experience, idea or event. (Keep this part short, and use the past tense.)

Example:

We were asked to work in pairs; and instead of being able to choose our own, the teacher chose the pairs,

which I thought was unfair as I ended up working with someone I wouldn't normally have chosen.

B   Think about how what you already know relates to the experience. (Use the present tense.)

Example:

I understand why the teacher grouped us this way, as previously we have chosen to work with our friends, and perhaps we needed to get a different perspective.

Also, some of the less confident students don't participate much in class discussions, so this enables them to voice their opinions, without putting them on the spot.

C   Consider how it went. (You can include emotions/feelings.)

Example:

Initially, I was worried we wouldn't come up with any ideas; we sat in silence for a few seconds, then Marta got out her notebook and started to draw a mind-map, as we discussed the issue.

We found we could bounce ideas off each other really well, and I was surprised to learn how much easier it was to remember things when you made notes like that.

CONTINUED

D Identify the part(s) which you think you learned the most from, why this was, and how you and others feel about it. (Part of reflection is discussing your feelings/thoughts with others and looking at things from different perspectives.)

Example:

> I'd never considered making notes like that before, and I really enjoyed it and learned from it, so it proved to be a useful strategy. For me, the most significant aspect was I felt as if I'd be able to remember the information better when we presented to the class next time. I always thought that I was more of a visual person and remembered by reading and looking, rather than by doing.

> Now I know better. Marta seems to think that if we look, hear and do, we'll improve our learning and memory. I think I agree with her now.

E Explain how your analysis of the experience, idea or event might affect your future learning. (This is explaining what you might need to do/learn to impact on your future learning, so will mostly use the future tense, i.e. you are predicting.)

Example:

> The knowledge I have gained from this experience is really useful as I can use this strategy in my future studies.

> My next step will be to look again at other situations where I can apply this strategy, discuss it with others in my group, and start to reflect on my learning more regularly. I will also look at some other blogs.

Now it's your turn!

1 For each of the five stages outlined above, record your own ideas based on an experience you have had. Use the examples given in the speech bubbles as a guide only, and replace them with your own words according to the experience you are reflecting on.

2 When you have discussed the experience and had further time to reflect on it, you can come back to your initial reflections and add to them, creating further successful reflections.

3 Now share your own versions of the speech bubbles in your group. As a group be ready to explain this strategy to the rest of the class. Did you find it helpful? Would you use this strategy yourselves?

Group D – Strategy 4: Gibbs' 'Reflective Cycle'

One way of looking at reflection is as a cycle. We reflect on past actions to improve our performance. You can follow Gibbs' strategy each time you want to reflect on something that has happened to you, as shown in Figure 8.3.

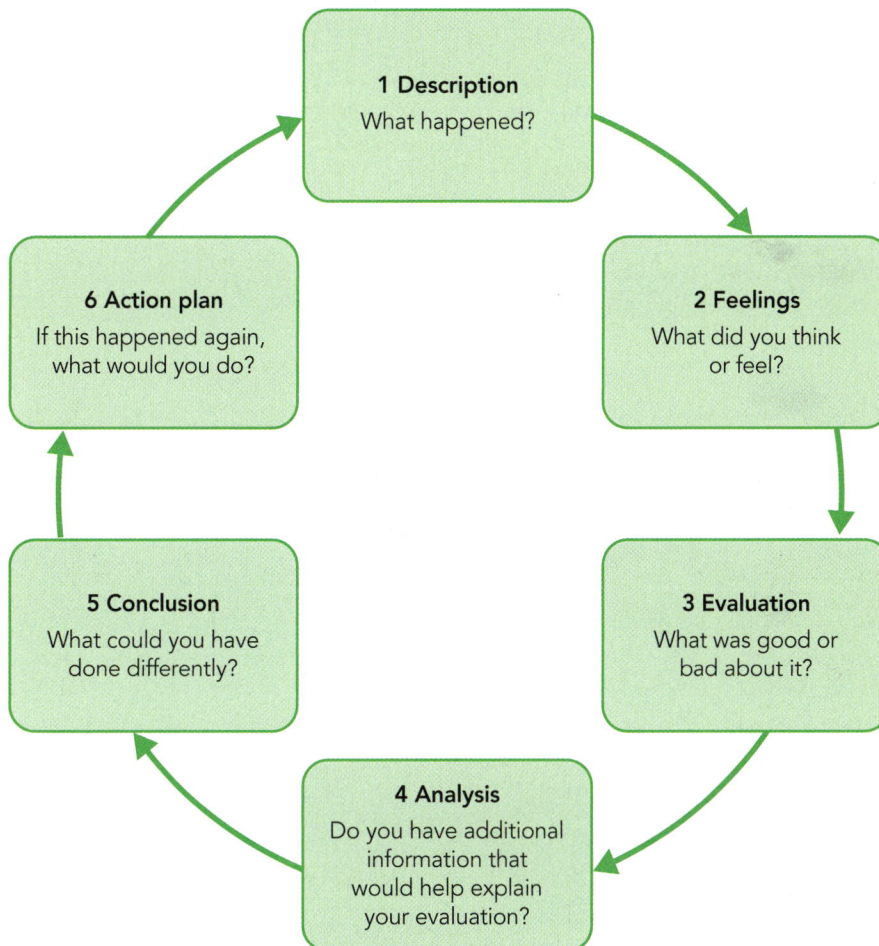

1 Description
What happened?

2 Feelings
What did you think or feel?

3 Evaluation
What was good or bad about it?

4 Analysis
Do you have additional information that would help explain your evaluation?

5 Conclusion
What could you have done differently?

6 Action plan
If this happened again, what would you do?

Figure 8.3: Gibbs' Reflective Cycle

1 Think about an experience you had at school or at home. Answer the questions in Figure 8.3 to help you reflect using Gibbs' Reflective Cycle.

2 Now share your answers to these questions with your group. As a group be ready to explain this strategy to the rest of the class. Did you find it helpful? Would you use this strategy yourselves?

> **REFLECTION**
>
> Now you have heard about four different strategies. With a partner, discuss all four. Were there any differences or similarities? Which would you use? Why? Do these strategies make you feel more confident about reflecting than you did before you started this section of the chapter?

8.2 Reflecting objectively on different perspectives

When you research a topic or an issue, you will find that different authors have different views and perspectives. Some may agree with your own views, and some may disagree. To make sure you have a clear basis for your own position on an issue, you have to try to be objective in your reading. This means you must read with an open mind and try to reflect on what the authors say, even when you might disagree with them initially. You may find that, following reflection, you decide you have to check on their perspectives by doing further research. Sometimes an excellent argument may be based on faulty information or the author's opinion and, just because you agree with them, that is not enough for you to be sure.

Figure 8.4: How much is too much salt in your diet?

ACTIVITY 8.02

While researching the topic Health and wellbeing, you discover that there is a debate about salt intake in the average diet (Figure 8.4).

1 Before you continue with this activity, write a short note about what you know about salt intake. Do you think people eat too much salt? Is this a problem?

2 Now read these two short texts about salt in the average diet. While you are reading, note down what the perspective and opinion of each writer is.

Source 1

Improving the eating habits of the population is important for the general health of society. High salt intake is a major problem, causing high blood pressure, stroke, and stomach cancer. 69% of adults in England are estimated to be eating too much salt, according to a government National Diet and Nutrition Survey in 2020.

Government policies should help people eat healthily, and this includes measuring the amount of salt that is within food and ensuring that there is not too much of it. Government strategies for reducing salt intake could include: creating policies to make sure food manufacturers produce healthier foods, raising awareness about the need to reduce salt intake through advertising and promoting healthy food in schools, workplaces, communities, and cities.

The government should legislate to make sure that the food industry reduces salt in products over time so that consumers get used to the taste and don't switch to alternative products. At the same time food manufacturers could be persuaded to promote the benefits of eating reduced salt foods through their advertisements to raise consumer awareness.

On a personal level, salt consumption at home can be reduced by not adding salt while preparing and cooking food, and by eating fewer salty snacks like crisps and peanuts.

Source: National Diet and Nutrition Survey (NDNS) 2020 study (www.gov.uk)

CONTINUED

Source 2

The National Academy of Medicine (NAM), USA, recommends a sodium intake of less than 2,300 mg per day, corresponding to 5.8 grams of salt. At the same time, some researchers (American Heart Association) think an intake between 3,000 and 5,000 mg of sodium per day is the best level. This is about average for the USA.

If your doctor advises you to limit your salt intake, you should do so of course. But if you are generally healthy, following a low salt diet will not help to improve your health. Eating too much salt may be dangerous to health, but too little salt can also be dangerous. Limiting salt intake can raise cholesterol, and has been linked with increased insulin resistance, a condition that increases blood sugar and insulin levels. This may lead to serious diseases.

Most of the excess salt we eat comes from salty snacks and processed food, which we should probably avoid anyway. Adding some salt to cooking and preparing healthy foods makes them taste nicer and is safe and healthy.

Sources:
National Academy of Medicine (nam.edu/on)
American Heart Association (pubmed.ncbi.nlm.nih.gov)

3   Now reflect on the two texts:

  a   How would you summarise the differences between their perspectives?

  b   Has reading the two perspectives changed your own perspective? Do you agree with one or the other? Or would you need to do some more research on the topic to decide if one or the other, or both are right?

8.3 Reflecting with empathy on others' perspectives

Reflecting on what you have learned can help you to remember it. Other people may have different perspectives because their lives and experiences are different from yours and it is helpful to think about the different ways they are affected by issues. When you listen to what someone else has to say about an issue, this can open your eyes to aspects of an issue you may not have thought about beforehand. This may be because they have different or more information, or because they are impacted differently.

You learned a little about empathy in Chapter 7. To really learn from others we have to listen to them with attention and empathy, to try to understand their situation, their feelings and why they think the way they do. Only then can we understand their perspective. We have to put aside our personal views and prejudices and pay attention to what they are communicating. In all areas of Cambridge Global Perspectives, we need to show that we can reflect on others' perspectives with empathy.

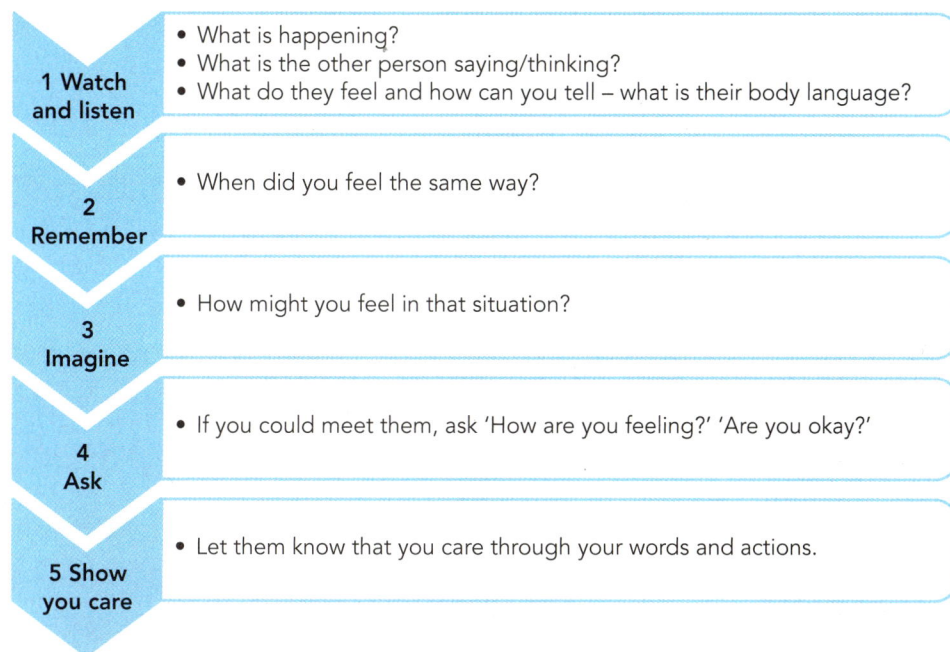

1 Watch and listen	• What is happening? • What is the other person saying/thinking? • What do they feel and how can you tell – what is their body language?
2 Remember	• When did you feel the same way?
3 Imagine	• How might you feel in that situation?
4 Ask	• If you could meet them, ask 'How are you feeling?' 'Are you okay?'
5 Show you care	• Let them know that you care through your words and actions.

Figure 8.5: Developing empathy

ACTIVITY 8.03

1   Below is the summary of a video clip on the topic of Education for all. Write down what you think the clip will be about and six words you think you might hear during the clip.

> For children growing up in refugee camps, education is a powerful tool of liberation. In this inspiring talk, Makhtoum Abdalla, displaced as a child in Sudan and now living with his family in the Otash camp in Darfur, shares his biggest dream: to ensure all children are educated and taught the skills needed to become 'captains of their destiny'.

2   The video clip is approximately ten minutes long. Watch and listen to the video clip. It is a TED talk called 'Education is a Fundamental Right for Every Child' by Makhtoum Abdalla. This talk was presented at a TED Salon event given in partnership with UNICEF. You can find it by typing 'ted talks Makhtoum Abdalla' into an internet search engine.

CONTINUED

3   Make notes to help you remember the key information in the video clip.

4   Combine the information you have found out from parts **1–3** to write down your detailed ideas on what the perspective is which is being presented by Makhtoum Abdalla.

5   In your group discuss what you have learned from this video clip, both in terms of information and in terms of the perspective of people with a different life experience. Is this perspective similar to or different from your own? Write down your reasons for your decision.

ACTIVITY 8.04

Conduct some research on indigenous communities like those shown in Figure 8.6. What topics or issues have you discovered that affect different indigenous people? What other questions do you have?

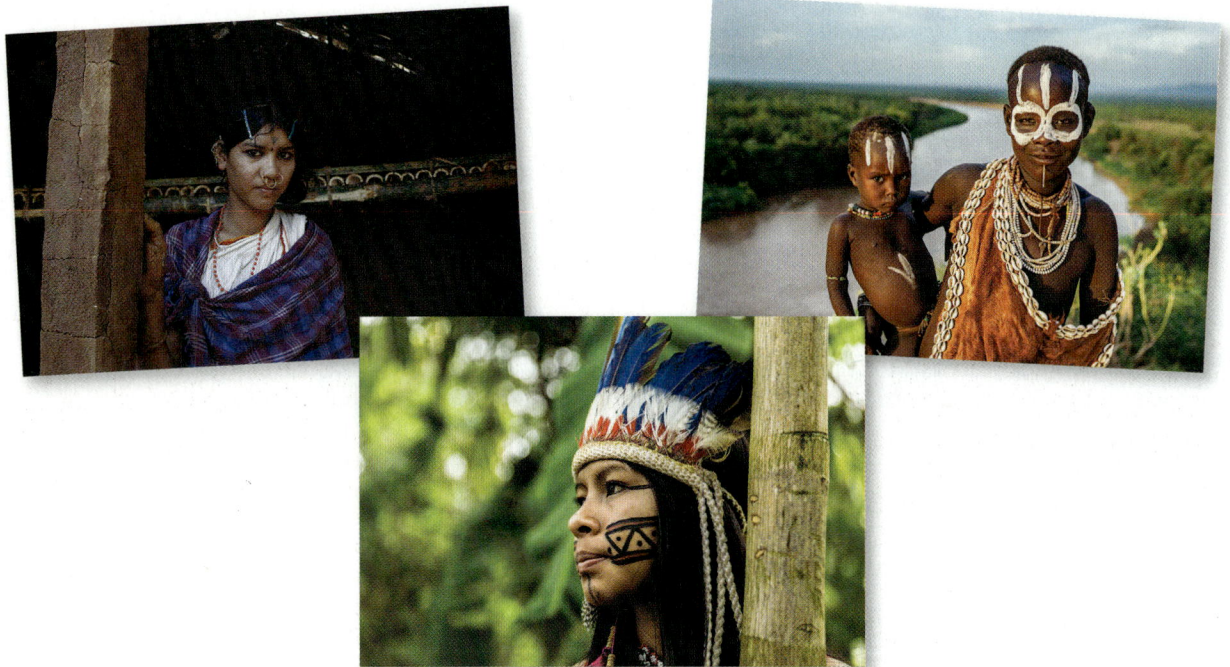

Figure 8.6: Indigenous people

1   Using the five steps in Figure 8.5, write answers to respond to the first three questions.

2   Chose an image. Work with a partner. One of you takes on the role of the person in the image and the other is the interviewer.

3   Role play the dialogue that might take place for all five steps of Figure 8.5.

4   Swap roles and conduct the role play again. Make sure you have both had a chance to play the role of the empathetic interviewer and the person in the image.

REFLECTION

- As the interviewer in Activity 8.04, which of you (you or your partner) showed more empathy?

- Why do you think this was?

ACTIVITY 8.05

1   Find a short interview between a reporter and someone from an indigenous community. You could try the search terms: 'interview' 'indigenous people'.

2   Listen to what the interviewer says. Write down examples of empathy that the interviewer uses.

3   Answer the following questions:

    a   Overall, how empathetic do you think the interviewer is to the situation of the person being interviewed?

    b   How do you think that the interviewer could be more empathetic?

4   Find a partner who has a different interview from yours. Share your interview and your thoughts about how empathetic the interviewer is with your partner. Which of the two interviewers do you think is more empathetic to the situation of the person being interviewed and why do you think this?

ACTIVITY 8.06

1   Below is the summary of a video clip. Like the video clip you watched in Activity 8.03 this clip addresses the topic Education for all. Read the summary and write down what you think the clip will be about and four issues you think might be covered during the clip.

> In the lead up to the G7 Summit and Global Partnership for Education replenishment summit, we are launching a global call to action to ensure no girl with disabilities is left behind. The UN Girls' Education Initiative joined forces with Leonard Cheshire, Sightsavers, VSO, Light for the World, and the Commonwealth Children and Youth Disability Network to advocate for more gender-responsive and inclusive education systems. Hear from girls and young women with disabilities, and inclusion advocates from around the world, sharing their recommendations to world leaders.

CONTINUED

2   Watch and listen to the video clip. It is approximately five minutes long. You can find it by visiting the website for the United Nations Girls' Education Initiative and using the search box to look for 'Girls with disabilities have an equal right to education'.

While you watch:

a   Try to imagine how the people on the video clip feel and listen to what they say with attention and empathy.

b   Take notes to help you remember the different perspectives you hear in the video clip.

After you have watched the clip discuss your impressions with a partner and write down the answers to these questions:

3   What are the main recommendations that were shared in the video clip?

4   How were your views on education affected by listening to and watching the girls and women in the video clip?

8.4 Justifying your own perspective using evidence and reasoning

When you have reflected both objectively and with empathy on other people's perspectives on an issue, you should come to a conclusion about your own perspective and be prepared to justify it to other people. When you want to convince others of your point of view (unless they already agree with you!) you must back up what you are saying with evidence and reasoning. You have to provide your listeners with reasons to accept your view. Without reasoning and evidence, your opinion will not stand up to any kind of debate. If anyone asks you a question, you will not be able to answer. The best way to win any debate is to have plenty of support for your perspective so that you are able to justify it. The same is true when you write an essay or write long answers to questions. Without evidence and reasoning your writing and answers will not be convincing.

TIP

Conveying a message persuasively requires strong communication skills. To help you develop these, make use of the guidance in Chapter 6; for example, Section 6.3 contains guidelines for preparing and giving presentations.

DISCUSSION

1   Think back to the two video clips you watched in Activities 8.03 and 8.06. What made these two clips convincing in their different ways? Note down a few ideas.

2   With your partner discuss what kind of evidence was provided in each of the clips. What reasoning was provided to support the perspective in each clip? What were the similarities and differences? Was one more convincing than the other?

Figure 8.7: Lawyers use evidence and reasoning to justify their perspective to the court

ACTIVITY 8.07

1   Choose one of the topics or issues below and decide what you think about it.

- Tourism: beneficial or damaging to our country?

- Personal car ownership: sustainable or not?

- Fast fashion provides work for vulnerable people.

- Renewable energy should be subsidised by the government.

- Students should be allowed to use electronic devices in the classroom.

- Should we stop deforestation?

- Should healthcare be provided free of charge to all citizens?

- Should we employ migrants when some citizens are unemployed?

- All new buildings should be designed and built to be sustainable.

- We need a larger police force and more prisons to reduce crime.

2   Find some evidence to support your view.

3   Think of two or three reasons why your perspective is right.

4   Prepare to present your perspective to the class. You can present in any way you prefer. Your presentation should not take longer than three minutes. You will have to justify your perspective by giving some evidence and explaining your reasons for thinking as you do. Just in case, be ready to answer some questions.

TIP

You could record your presentation to show to the class (you could record it on a phone or some other electronic device); or write your ideas out and read them to the class, or prepare a slideshow with two or three slides to talk the class through, or any other method of presentation you like. If you would like to work with a partner that is also okay.

8.5 Reflecting with balance and empathy on your experience of working in a team

When you have finished work on a team project that involved carrying out your action, you should reflect on and evaluate:

- the benefits and challenges of working as a team

- the strengths and weaknesses of your own performance as a team member

- your learning about the issue from your research, your team members' research and others' perspectives

- what you learned about your own skills from working on the project

- the action your team took – whether it helped to achieve the project aims, fully, partially, or not at all.

- your own work processes – your personal strengths and weaknesses in your research and in carrying out your own responsibilities.

You should also suggest what could have been done better or differently, in terms of both the action the team took and your own work processes. These suggestions should be based on the weaknesses you identified as part of your reflection.

These reflections can be written down in what is called a 'reflective paper'. When writing down your reflection in a reflective paper, keep in mind that, in addition to covering the points above, your paper should:

- be well structured, and easy to understand

- present your own research findings

- include citations and referencing as appropriate.

> **TIP**
>
> When writing a reflective paper you can draw on the research and writing skills that you have developed in Chapters 5 and 6.

Figure 8.8: Team work benefits from reflection on the whole project

Now you are going to work on reflecting on teamwork.

1 Look at the bullet list at the start of the section and decide which items on the list will be easy to do and which ones will be more difficult. Make a note of those.

2 Discuss your thoughts with a partner. Did you agree? How could you show balance and empathy when writing about teamwork?

3 Now, on your own, read the information below about a team project carried out by a group of learners. It is followed by two different team members' reflections on their own strengths and weaknesses as a team member.

Aim: To raise money for a local charity who give food and shelter to the homeless

Action: A poster campaign to persuade people of the importance of giving donations to charities who help provide food and shelter to homeless people

Example A – Reflection on own performance as a team member

I personally found this a very rewarding experience. My main contribution to our team's project was creating the survey that we gave out to get responses to inform our poster outcome. I was also able to contribute in other ways like making the list of people who we wanted to view our poster campaign. I should have been able to work more quickly but I took my time. I felt that this might have been a weakness, but it didn't seem to have much effect on our progress.

CONTINUED

Example B – Reflection on own performance as a team member

It is hard to write this part of the reflective paper, because of my personal experience. However, I will be realistic about the strength of my contribution. My contribution was the project itself. The other team members couldn't cope with the given tasks – one was silent and the other was absent. Therefore, I contributed by formulating and writing a plan with limited help from team members. I researched all the information needed for the production of the outcome, again with only a little help from one other team member. I contacted sources to show different cultural perspectives in the outcome and I wrote the explanation of the project. Finally, I produced most of the outcome. One of the posters was completed by another team member, but this wasn't very good and we didn't include it in our final submission. I feel that I have made far more contribution and effort to work in class and outside of class time to complete the project than anyone else in my team.

The weakness of my contribution was that I lacked the ability to lead and communicate with my team members. I feel that if I had tried harder to communicate with my team members about the problems they were facing completing the given tasks, I might not have had to do so much work myself at the end.

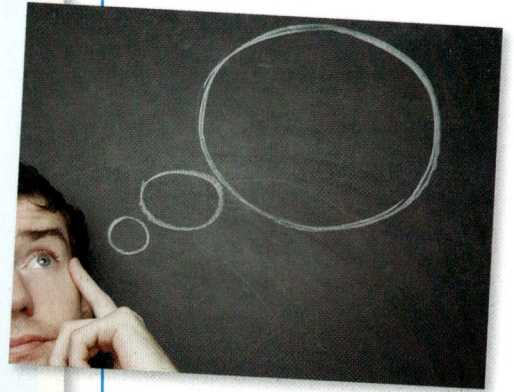

4   Which of these two examples do you think is better at sharing their reflection on their own strengths and weaknesses as a team member? What makes it better? Note down your ideas to share.

5   With a partner, share your thoughts on the two examples. Discuss how you might improve Example A.

Make a few notes of your ideas so that you remember them when you come to writing your own reflective paper.

As well as reflecting on your own performance as a team member, your strengths and weaknesses and how you interacted with the other members of your team, you should think about the whole experience of team work. What are the advantages of working in a team and what are the challenges?

ACTIVITY 8.09

1   Read the following example of part of a reflective paper that discusses a team project and notice the parts that are about teamwork. While you read, think about the following questions and jot down your thoughts:

a   Is there a balance of benefits and challenges of teamwork?

b   Is there some evaluation?

c   Is there too much/too little description of things that happened?

Reflective paper (extract)

I was put in a team with four other students: Jamil, Nimish, Marc and Zain. I did not know them very well. We met as a group to decide on a local problem, and we soon agreed on that. We decided to focus on local access to healthcare as we think that is a problem for lots of different people in the area. Our families have had some problems with this, so probably people who are poorer would have more of a problem. We also agreed what each one of us would research. I agreed to find out about the perspective of medical experts, probably a local doctor and a nurse at the local health centre, or maybe some people working at the hospital. The others agreed to research how other groups feel about the problem and what their experiences are. Also Nimish decided to research what has been done in other countries to solve this problem, or whether there have been successful campaigns about access to health care. Nimish and I did most of the talking and the others seemed to be very quiet and did not join in the discussions much. I felt a bit angry about this because it meant I was not sure if the others would really do their work or if they really understood what we had agreed to do. We agreed to keep in touch during the week and to meet the week after to share our research findings and to see what we could do for our action.

I got a couple of messages from Nimish, and we kept in touch about what we had done, but got no answers or messages from the others. When we met to share our findings, it turned out that one of the others, Marc, had not done any research at all and he did not seem bothered about it. He just said he was not interested so he didn't research. Jamil and Zain had

CONTINUED

both done some research by asking their family members. I had been to the local clinic and interviewed a doctor there and his assistant nurse, as I promised. Unfortunately Jamil and Zain had asked family members who were also doctors, so we did not have a range of perspectives and had to do some more research after. We will try to ask some of the cleaning staff at the school about their experiences in getting healthcare. Anyhow we agreed that we would do a campaign of raising awareness of the problem of access to healthcare in our town. We checked with the teacher, and she got permission from the principal for us to give a presentation to parents and students from our class about the problem. We decided to do two different things, one a presentation about the information we find out and then a little role play about different perspectives of people we have interviewed. Marc promised to interview some of the cleaners at school, and we decided to use that information and Nimish's findings to write a role play about different perspectives.

Working in a team can be really difficult when you don't know each other well. Chatty people like me and Nimish could do too much talking and people like Marc might not get involved because they are not sure what is going on. That meant that we didn't get ourselves properly organised as a team. We didn't really discuss enough in the beginning, and we just agreed with Zain's idea when she mentioned it, and Nimish and I talked too much. But it is also quite a good experience to work with other people. We did get ourselves sorted out the second time we met, and we managed to be more organised and listen properly to each other. That was really good because then we found out that people had some different ideas to solve the problems we had. When we listened properly to Marc, and asked him what he thought, he got interested and came up with some really good ideas about the role play. I think the real problem was that we were not comfortable the first time we met, so we rushed everything and did not get to know each other first or discuss things in detail. That was why we ended up with people not keeping in touch and also researching the same perspective.

2   With a partner, or in a group, share your thoughts about the experiences of the team in the example above. Why did their first meeting not go too well? What do you think they did in their second meeting that helped everyone to get involved? Could they have done things differently in their first meeting to avoid the misunderstandings?

As you can see in the reflective paper in Activity 8.09, things did not always go to plan for this team. However, this piece of writing has some points of improvement that could be considered:

1   More detail was needed about the planning of the project tasks – who was going to do what and when it was due. The writing seemed to blame certain people, which did not show empathy.

2   Too much emphasis was placed on how the group interacted, rather than on what they were researching and why. The author could have suggested ways that they could have addressed the communication issues as part of the reflection.

3   The author does not write in enough detail about their own contribution to the teamwork or what they learned from doing the project.

4   The reflection does not show the team's progress from the start to the end of the project. The reflective paper could have written about how the skill of collaboration improved or how the research they conducted got better as the project progressed.

When you are writing your own reflective paper you should keep these points in mind as you begin to write.

Figure 8.9: Cambridge Global Perspectives gives you steps that can open future doors

SHOWCASING YOUR SKILLS

Reflection

Look at the guidance for writing a reflective paper in Section 8.5.

In Chapter 7 you carried out a team project with your group. You did some reflection on that at the end of the chapter in the reflection and review section.

Now, with the notes you took while studying Chapter 7, write a reflective paper on the team project you carried out.

Make sure you plan the paper so that you do not miss out any aspects of your reflection. Remember to give references for any sources you used in your individual research.

Reflection on the showcase

Write a few lines describing what went well.

Did you include everything that was required? How do you know?

What was difficult?

How could you improve things for next time?

Did you enjoy reflecting on the team project?

Did this activity help you to improve your skill of reflection?

SUMMARY

In Chapter 8 you have been thinking about and practising skills of reflection.

You have studied different reflection strategies and practised applying some of these. You have practised reflecting objectively and with empathy on different perspectives and on your own experience of working as part of a team, including the benefits and challenges that teamwork brings. You have considered how your own learning and perspectives are affected by research and others' perspectives and thought about how to justify your own perspective.

You have also thought about the benefits and challenges of working in a team and practised writing a reflective paper on a team project.

REVIEW OF LEARNING

	I have learned about …	I need more practice with …
Different strategies for reflecting		
Reflecting objectively on different perspectives		
Reflecting on other people's perspectives with empathy		
Justifying my own perspective using evidence and reasoning		
Reflecting on my experience of working as a team		

> Glossary

access to information/knowledge: this can be part of expertise. It is concerned with what a source knows or can find out. Do they have the information already, if not, can they get the information?

acronym: an abbreviation formed from the initial letters of other words and pronounced as a word.

active listening: the process in which the listener takes active responsibility to understand the content and feeling of what is being said and then checks with the speaker to see if they heard what the speaker intended to communicate.

analyse: to examine something in detail to understand what it is and how it is constructed.

analysis: studying or examining the parts of something, or the details, to understand it better.

anecdotal evidence: evidence in the form of stories people tell about their experiences.

argument: a series of statements containing reasons and evidence which support a claim about a global issue.

assume: to think something is true or is certain to happen, without checking if we are right.

bias: showing an inclination or prejudice for or against one person or group, especially in a way considered to be unfair.

bibliography: a list of sources referred to in a report or essay printed at the end of the written work.

chunking: breaking down information into smaller, more manageable pieces.

citing: quoting from or mentioning a particular author or a publication when you use their material, in the main body of the work.

claim: a statement that something is true.

cohesive: fitting together well, each part following logically, so that a reader can read through and follow the whole argument. Each paragraph should be cohesive, and each paragraph should follow on logically from the last one, making the whole essay cohesive.

collaboration: working together with others in a supportive and effective way.

communication: sharing ideas, feelings or information with others by speaking, in writing or in any other way.

conclusion: a reasoned judgement, a result, a final summary. You can come to a conclusion about something when you have looked at the evidence. You can also write a conclusion at the end of an essay, when you sum up your argument and answer the question.

context: background, setting or circumstances that surround an idea or a statement and help you to understand it better.

convention: a custom or a way of acting or doing something that is widely accepted and followed.

copyright: a law that gives the owner of a written document, music, book or picture the right to decide what can be done with it. If work is copyrighted, it can only be copied with permission from the author.

counter argument: an argument or set of reasons opposing an idea that is presented in another argument.

course of action: a plan or method used for achieving a specific aim or goal.

credibility: the credibility of a source refers in general to how believable the author is and how much we can rely on what they say.

debate: a formal discussion on a particular issue in a public meeting, in which opposing arguments are put forward and which usually ends in a vote.

dictation: saying something aloud for someone else to write down in order to create a record of it.

economic: about money.

effective listening: listening to the words of the speaker and the meaning of the words.

empathy: the experience of understanding and sharing another person's feelings from their perspective. You place yourself 'in their shoes' and imagine what they are feeling.

ethics: principles of what is right and wrong, for example when conducting an activity like research.

evaluate: to identify/assess the strengths and weaknesses of something.

evaluation: working out if something is useful, valuable, effective, by looking at its good points and its bad points, or its strengths and weaknesses.

evidence: information about a global issue that helps to develop understanding or prove that something is true or false.

experience: practical knowledge or skills learned over time and with practice or from life events. Most skills can be improved with practice, and we can learn from the things that happen to us. You might trust someone who has experience with your problem.

expertise: the skill of an expert. Expertise can be gained by study, training or experience, or a combination of all of these. You might trust someone who is trained to do a job more than someone who has no training or has not studied the area.

fact: something that is known or can be proved to be true.

fallacy: an error in reasoning or a mistaken idea.

gist: the general meaning of a piece of text.

global perspective: a perspective about the whole world, or planet Earth.

globalisation: the development of close connections between all (or most) of the countries in the world, building closer economic, cultural and political relations between them. This is happening because communication and travel are easier now.

indigenous: indigenous people are groups who are connected by ancestry to a particular geographical area.

inequality: in a social context, the fact that some people or groups or countries have more opportunities, money, resources, power than other people, groups or countries.

interview: a meeting where a researcher can obtain information by asking questions.

issue: an important subject or problem for discussion.

justify: to prove or give a good reason for something.

local perspective: a perspective about a local area or the views of a local community.

logical: sensible and reasonable.

metacognition: thinking about learning more explicitly, often by selecting a suitable strategy for planning, monitoring or evaluation of learning.

national perspective: a perspective about a particular country, or common to a whole country (it could be a view of the country given by one person, or a common view of many people in the country).

opinion: a personal belief or idea that may or may not be correct.

paragraph: a section of writing containing one main idea or part of an argument, presented in a clear and logical way.

personal perspective: someone's own view about an issue, usually how it affects them personally.

perspective: a viewpoint on an issue based on evidence and reasoning.

plagiarism: intentionally or unintentionally copying the words and phrases of someone else and presenting them as your own work.

Pomodoro technique: a method for timing work in set intervals with built-in breaks.

prediction: a statement about what might happen in the future.

primary data: information collected directly, for example through questionnaires, surveys or interviews.

primary source: an original document or object giving an account of the event or topic being researched.

proofread: the last thing you do before declaring a piece of written work is 'finished'. Pay attention to your grammar. Correct all the spelling errors, especially the ones that spell-checking misses (such as 'there'/'their', and 'to'/'too').

proposal: something (for example a claim or statement) that is put forward for consideration.

questionnaire: a set of written questions with a choice of answers that can be used to collect information from a large number of people.

reasoning: thinking in a clear and sensible way. In writing, reasoning means a series of justifications that support an author's perspective or argument.

reference: when you give a reference in a piece of written work, you acknowledge the use of a source of information that you used.

reflection: thinking deeply. This could be about something that has happened, something you have learned, or how to get your own ideas and feelings clear in your own mind.

relevant: directly connected with, appropriate to.

reliability: the trustworthiness of evidence. You might decide the information in a source is reliable because it has proved to be reliable in other circumstances, or because others have told you it is reliable.

reputation: what people say or think about a person or an organisation. If someone has a good reputation, you might trust them and, also, they might be honest because they want to keep their good reputation.

research: the systematic study of a global issue to find evidence and develop understanding.

research methods: the methods used to gather data and information that will be used in your work to support the points you make.

revise: to re-read a text and make changes (in content, organisation, sentence structures and word choice) to improve it. During revision, you may want to add, remove, move and/or substitute text.

scan: to look quickly at a text, without reading it, to find certain details.

secondary data: information from published sources on the internet, in newspapers, magazines, journals or books.

secondary source: gives information about a primary source. This information may cover the same topic but has been collected and arranged from a number of different sources.

self-aware: aware of your own character, feelings, motives and desires.

SMART plan: a plan that is specific, measurable, achievable, relevant and timely.

social: about people/society.

solution: a means of solving a problem or dealing with a difficult situation.

sound: in the context of a disagreement, an argument that is convincing because it has reasons and evidence that effectively support its conclusions.

standpoint: a point of view, attitude, position, way of thinking or perspective.

statistics: numerical data collected and analysed for the purpose of evidence in support of claims for arguments.

supporting sentence: a sentence that gives information, an explanation and/or examples to support the topic sentence.

survey: a research method used to collect data from a specific set of people to gain insights and information on a topic.

sustainable living: a lifestyle that attempts to reduce an individual's or society's use of the Earth's natural resources and personal resources.

tone: a quality in the voice of the speaker that expresses the speaker's feelings or thoughts, often towards the person being spoken to or the topic being spoken about. It can also refer to expressions of mood in music.

topic sentence: the sentence that expresses the main idea in a paragraph; usually the first sentence in the paragraph.

value judgement: a personal judgement about whether something is good or bad, right or wrong, based on personal beliefs or values.

values: moral principles/ideas/beliefs/feelings about what is morally correct, right, good or desirable.

verifying: making sure that something is true, accurate or justified.

vested interest: a personal reason for being involved in a project or situation, especially if it is for financial gain or recognition from others.

> Acknowledgements

The authors and publishers acknowledge the following sources of copyright material and are grateful for the permissions granted. While every effort has been made, it has not always been possible to identify the sources of all the material used, or to trace all copyright holders. If any omissions are brought to our notice, we will be happy to include the appropriate acknowledgements on reprinting.

Unit 3 Abridged extract from 'Indigenous peoples' published and used with the permission of Amnesty International; **Unit 4** Adapted extract from 'New evidence that fast food is bad for kids learning' by Kabir Chibber in Quartz, 21 December 2014, reproduced with permission of Quartz Media Inc.; Adapted extract from 'Europe must take responsibility in migration crisis: Parliament head' from Daily Sabah, November 2021; Abridged extract from 'What vegan propaganda ignores' by John Lewis-Stempel in Unherd, 5 January, 2022, reproduced with the permission of Unherd Ltd.; Abridged extract from 'Net zero 2050: new aircraft technology' published and used with permission of International Air Transport Association (IATA); Adapted extract 'Stay grounded' from 'Going Green – Are you thinking of making great escape with summer break?' by Chris Page, Edinburgh Evening News, January 2022, used with the permission of Angela Terry - One Home; **Unit 5** Adapted extract from 'Why fresh water shortages will cause the next great global crisis' by Robin McKie in The Guardian, 8 March 2015, Copyright Guardian News & Media Ltd.; Abridged extract from 'The United Nations Convention on the Rights of the Child from 1990', used with the permission of World Vision Canada; **Unit 6** Adapted extract from 'Globalisation: good or bad?' by Lewis Williamson in The Guardian, 31 October 2002, Copyright Guardian News & Media Ltd.; Adapted extract from 'Migration crisis: Who can refuse these human beings? Who?' asks a UN official' by Sam Jones in The Guardian, 4 Sept 2015, Copyright Guardian News & Media Ltd.; Adapted extract from 'Does migration change life for the better for people from poor countries?' by Claire Provost in The Guardian, 13 September 2013, Copyright Guardian News & Media Ltd.; Adapted extract from 'Why we promote Sustainable living' published and used with the permission of WWF, https://www.wwf.org.uk/what-we-do/promoting-sustainable-living © WWF-UK. All rights reserved; **Unit 8** Adapted extract from 'Court of Arbitration for Sport ignored anti-doping code in Valieva ruling, says WADA' by Steve Keating and Julien Pretot, used with the permission of Reuters © 2022 Reuters. All rights reserved; Adapted extract from 'Girls with disabilities have an equal right to education' published and used with the permission of UNGEI.

Thanks to the following for permission to reproduce images:

Cover FredFroese/GI; *Inside* **Unit 1** Artur Debat/GI; Matthias Kulka/GI; Aldra/GI; Larry Washburn/GI; Hinterhaus Productions/GI; Hispanolistic/GI; Grant Faint/GI; Marco Bottigelli/GI; Jose Luis Pelaez Inc/GI; NurPhoto/GI; Kali9/GI; Catherine Falls Commercial/GI; Imaginima/GI; **Unit 2** Klaus Vedfelt/GI; Sean Gladwell/GI; DrAfter123/GI; DDDB/GI; Kirill Perchenko/GI; Vladimir Godnik/GI; Digital Vision/GI; Hispanolistic/GI; SDI Productions/GI; Yuji Sakai/GI; **Unit 3** Andriy Onufriyenko/GI; South_agency/GI; RuslanDashinsky/GI; Felipe Dupouy/GI; Bryant Scannell/GI; Hadynyah/GI(x2); Grandriver/GI; Richard Drury/GI; Fuse/GI; Izusek/GI; Westend61/GI; Chris Upson/GI; **Unit 4** Georgeclerk/GI; Yagi Studio/GI; Maskot/GI; Leon Neal/GI; Mayur Kakade/GI; MikeyGen73/GI; Andriy Onufriyenko/GI; Sabrina Mundl/GI; D76 Masahiro Ikeda/GI; FatCamera/GI; Pinstock/GI; 'AirbusZeroE Blendedwing Conceptplanes B2' from Airbus Media Centre; Peter Cade/GI; **Unit 5** Blackred/GI; Enviromantic/GI; Mint Images/GI; Deepak Sethi/GI; Tommy/GI; Bartosz Hadyniak/GI; Pablohart/GI; GCShutter/GI; Peter Dazeley/GI; Sparky/GI; Marko Geber/GI; Peter Dazeley/GI; Mareen Fischinger/GI; **Unit 6** Evgeny Tchebotarev/GI; SolStock/GI; Peter Cade/GI; Klaus Vedfelt/GI; Mayur Kakade/GI; Hill Street Studios/GI; Lisa5201/GI; Incamerastock/Alamy Stock Photo; GCShutter/GI; FilippoBacci/GI; Spyros Arsenis/GI; Rebecca Van Ommen/GI; Monty Rakusen/GI; Stockbyte/GI; Grant Faint/GI; **Unit 7** Antonio M. Rosario/GI; Prostock-Studio/GI; Rayman/GI; Blanscape/GI; track5/GI; Robert Nickelsberg/GI; Microgen Images/GI; Natalie Fobes/GI; Fotosearch/GI; Caia Image/GI; Marchiez/GI; Peter Muller/GI; Richard Drury/GI; **Unit 8** Andrea Comi/GI; WOWstockfootage/GI; Ian Hooton/GI; NurPhoto/GI; Hadynyah/GI; Filipefrazao/GI; Chris Ryan/GI; Stuart Fox/GI; Mattjeacock/GI; Yaorusheng/GI; Mike Powell/GI

Key GI = Getty Images